A Cherokee Feast of Days

A CHEROKEE
FEAST
OF DAYS

Daily Meditations

JOYCE SEQUICHIE HIFLER

Di Ka No He SGi-Di Go We Li SGi
(SHE WHO WRITES HER PHILOSOPHY ON PAPER)

COUNCIL OAK BOOKS

© 1992 by Joyce Sequichie Hifler
All rights reserved
96 95 94   5
ISBN 0-933031-65-3 Cloth
ISBN 0-933031-68-8 Paper
LC Number 91-77973

COUNCIL OAK BOOKS
1350 E. FIFTEENTH STREET
TULSA, OKLAHOMA 74120

DESIGNED BY CAROL HARALSON

THE AUTHOR WISHES TO ACKNOWLEDGE with deep appreciation the friendship and help of the late Mildred Milam Viles, daughter of a Cherokee chief, who supplied American Indian quotations from her extensive library in Claremore, Oklahoma.

This will also acknowledge the University of Oklahoma Press for its permission to quote from *The Cherokees*, authored by another longtime friend, the late Grace Steele Woodward of Tulsa. Portions of this work are taken from the author's nationally syndicated newspaper column, *Think on these Things*.

The Cherokee words and phrases are phonemic translations from the Cherokee syllabary which was given to the Cherokee people about 1821 by Cherokee genius Sequoyah. Several dialects change the spelling and pronunciations.

To my husband, Charles J. Zofness
To my daughter, Jane Hifler
To my Friend and Counselor,
The Great Holy Spirit

THE AMERICAN INDIAN LOVED A FEAST long before the Pilgrims came to dinner. When missionaries came to tell them about the crucified Jesus, the Chief stood up and said, "No! We did not do this thing! This Jesus sound like fine warrior. If He come to us, we ask him to sit down and feast with us." This is an invitation to come sit down for the Feast of Days that begins new every morning. When the sun breaks through the far side of the woods and sprays gold beneath ancient oaks, it is time to turn over a new leaf and celebrate a new beginning. The way of the Cherokee is to know the past is gone. Though a golden thread still links us to it in many ways, it no longer holds us captive, no longer keeps our feet on the Trail of Tears. We have new wisdom and understanding, and we dare to put down yesterday to reach for a new day. Whenever we sit with those who do not feast, we study to be quiet, take care of business, work with our hands and rejoice in our spirits. The best is yet to come.

JANUARY

Unu la ta nee'
Cold Month

*The Cherokee people stand upon new
ground. Let us hope the clouds which
overspread the land will be dispersed,
and that we shall prosper as we have
never before done.*

CHIEF JOHN ROSS
OCTOBER 9, 1861

January 1

If, like a Cherokee warrior, I can look at the new year as an opportunity to stand on new ground, then strength and courage are on my side. If I have waited a long time for everything to be perfect—and there have been moments, brief as they were, that filled my expectations—then I can face the challenges. I will remember that things do work out, bodies do heal, relationships mend—not because I said it, but because I believe it. But it is time to make things right, to stay on the path. As water runs fresh and free from the woodland spring, so new life and meaning will bubble up from my own inner source. I will be still and steady, because there is nothing to be gained by showing fear in a chaotic world. I can turn from ignorance and prejudice toward a light that never goes out.

The death of fear is in doing what you fear to do.
SEQUICHIE COMINGDEER

January 2

This morning, snow wrapped every tree and rock in soft white, and promised to keep the outline of distant hills hidden against a gray sky. But it could not keep its promise. After a few hours the sun came out and turned it all into nature's jewelry, beautiful dew gems sparkling on the grass. We can be so busy that we miss the little things that sweeten life, the way a pet waits to be noticed, the way an owl, a *wahuhi*, hoots in the woods, and a bluejay chortles in the middle of winter. It is a lovely thing to turn away from busy work to pay attention to our loved things and loved ones. We know how we wait to be told we are important. We should never wait to say or think something beautiful that will make someone's day easier and more secure.

We do not want riches. We want peace and love.
RED CLOUD 1870

January 3

When we last saw Essie she had been ashen and without the strength we see in her now. Now she sits flat on the ground, legs straight out in front, and reeds tumble across her knees and lie around her. Nimble fingers seek the perfect one to start a basket. Essie is close to our hearts. She has our Grandmother's name. Her reticence does not inspire idle talk, so we ask what happened to change her. With a quick glance, she says, "God heal." "Is it possible? So quickly and completely?" Hesitantly, she asks, "You got fast oven?" I say I do. "What make it work?" "Why, microwaves—energy. They change the molecules, the structure of the bread from cold to hot." Seconds pass. She says, almost too softly, "Prayer energy. Make me well."

I love a people who have always made me welcome to the best they had . . . who are honest without laws . . . who never take the name of God in vain . . . who worship God without a Bible . . . and I believe God loves them too.

GEORGE CATLIN, ARTIST 1830

January 4

To the Cherokee, worry is the *dalala,* the woodpecker, pecking away on the roof. It is easy to understand that even new wood cannot bear such hammering without giving way. Imagine what would happen to a roof which has already been through storms and many hot summers. But how do we handle this woodpecker called worry? By seeing it for what it is—a bird that causes damage. We can shout and scare it away for awhile, but as soon as we drop our guard it is back again. Worry did not crash in suddenly. It entered our lives little by little, so that we did not notice. Surely it will go away, but it takes its toll so gradually that we grow accustomed to it—thinking it is just a normal part of living. When we hear worry rapping on the roof, we can ask ourselves, what have we talked about? What have we heard or dwelled on that distresses us?

Udadolisdi nuwhtohiyada Jalagi. Cherokee pray for peace.

January 5

Nothing is so bedraggled and beaten down as a garden in winter. It promises nothing, and shows only wilted, gray and soggy leaves. There are no straight defined rows, no hint of green to show that it will ever be any different. But the Cherokee knows the difference. Long before winter—in the season of planting, we sowed the best seeds we could. As tiny and insignificant as they look, they will produce. When the best is planted and watered and cared for, the time will come to see the increase—to see a miracle. Life can be renewed and restored. Bedraggled and ridden down as life can be, don't despair. Plant good words, plant good seed. Nurture them with warm attention and care. Be a perennial believer and watch those first warm rays of sunlight awaken your garden to the Season of the Green Corn.

Sweet grasses and seeds serve as perfume for body and spirit.

INDIAN IMPRINTS

January 6

Dare to believe in miracles. Look beyond the mud on the windshield, beyond the impossible, and know life is more than anguish and stress. Reach out to someone, when your heart is too heavy to feel the sunlight or to taste the rain. Rid yourself of dark thought and melancholy. Open your mind to fresh air, to the unlimited music in your soul. Thoreau wrote of waking in the night to hear a strain of music dying away—travelers singing. He said his whole being was so expanded and infinitely and divinely related that he knew how narrow his own thinking had been. The Cherokee always teach their young to listen. We hear not the crash of cymbals or the noise that rides the airwaves—but the sweet song of the meadow, the even rhythmic sounds of nature. It is here where the *dikanowadidohi* angel sings.

Speak to yourself in spiritual songs, singing and making melody in your heart to the Lord.

January 7

The earth is too small for all the lonely people to have missed each other so completely. But the voice of loneliness seems to persist and deepen with every hour. The Cherokee elder teaches the young person, "Learn to know and like yourself. Learn to be your own best friend." Learn the art of enjoyable solitude—of having lunch with yourself and being comfortable about it. A person alone is unique. A lonely person shows it in his haunted stare. Sometimes loneliness comes because we have not made room for anyone else. We need to stretch beyond our boundaries, step out of familiar territory, stop nursing emptiness and self-indulgence. Loneliness is looking for something to fill a void. Joy is expanding so that others want to share our lives.

May your way be blessed with life by the unifying force of the Great Holy Spirit.

CHEROKEE PRAYER

January 8

Lo, the poor Indian!
Whose untutored mind
Sees God in clouds,
Or hears him in the wind.

Alexander Pope recognized the simplicity in the Indian's beliefs. Though all tribes are rich in symbolism to express what they believe, we all basically believe in One God, One Creator, One Great Loving Spirit over all. The Cherokees had their Father-Creator who was *Yowah*, the unity of three beings. The name *Yowah* was so sacred that only certain priests were allowed to say it. This same innate belief lives in each of us if we can only uncover it. Worship is of the heart, deep, joyous, personal. It is a life-current between each of us and our Creator. We can wrongly destroy ourselves but never the love that is beyond our understanding. It is there, even when we are too stubborn to receive it.

We perceive a battle between good and evil, and we also perceive good will win.
THE IROQUOIS

January 9

Sometimes great distances exist between the high points of our lives. Time moves swiftly and we tend to let it slip away without making it count while we wait on another high experience. We discount it as nothing unless we have reached some spectacular height and have passed ten other people on the way. The Indian does not consider himself idle when he stands still watching, listening, seeing the stars, or watching the sunset. His spirit-eyes absorb these signs and wonders to feed him when he cannot see the rolling hills, the flowing streams. A narrow view is one that constantly asks, What shall I eat? What shall I wear? What can make me feel secure? And all the time, the beauty and peace which cost nothing surround us unnoticed. Envy and lack of inner joy rob us of our peace of mind.

0, listen! Hear! Sing with me, for I am joy.

CHEROKEE SONG

January 10

When something in our minds rings a bell that warns us, we do well to listen. What is it that wants to lure us away from the chosen path? Is it not from the good side? Then, run like a rabbit! Every one of us has a sounding board, a testing place that detects the way we are moving. Like a compass, it points the right way—and we are foolish not to understand—*gohlga*. To ignore the impressions that are within us is like trying to go through a door, but refusing to use the doorknob. It is one thing to be dense and another to be willfully determined to get lost in the wilderness. Listen to the alarm system. It is there for a good reason—and later on we won't have to say that something told us not to go a certain way and we didn't listen.

He hears voices others do not hear; sees visions that confirm his dreams.

EAGLE OLD MAN

January 11

The owls call to each other early on a mid-winter evening. Just as the last rays of sunlight sink into a rosy glow, a silence settles over the countryside. For a short time, everything is hushed. In that near-dark hour the wind lays and no sound is heard—as though the whole forest listens. The moment is brief as daytime creatures find their nests and those of the night begin to awaken. It is time to rest from our own activity, to find a quiet hour to let pressures ebb away. One of the greatest wonders is the rhythm and order of nature. But even greater is the flexibility of human nature—that we can move, think, project, plan and see all of it in perspective. And as the day wanes we can put it all down and take on the peace of nature.

Heed little the melancholy nights that keep tune with sorrowful thought.
CHIEF RUNS-THE-BATTLE

January 12

As time goes by we learn it isn't the speed with which we do our work, but the quality of time that makes life an accomplishment. How much do we enjoy working, or playing, or just resting? Schedules and deadlines take up most of what we do. We seldom have time to enjoy something for the sake of doing it. If we feel pressured, we have little incentive to enjoy doing anything, much less doing it well. Many who have to sit all day are bored and have nothing to think about except how unhappy they are or how they feel physically. More time is not the answer. We need a better quality of life, *i ga osi,* deeper rest, and it begins with quality attitudes. What we have or what we do not have should never dictate the quality of our lives, or our capacity to simply enjoy.

Some pass without recognition, the grandest of all . . .
    SONG OF LOVE

January 13

Ifwe are not happy, it is because no one has given us permission to be. The hardships and stresses of those who went before us make us wonder if we have a right to do better. Do we have permission to outlive, outdo, outwork all those who went before us? Have we given our children permission to be stronger, better, and more intelligent than we are? The Cherokees have a word for it, *adahnehdi*, meaning the gift. Or have we told them to adhere to their roots instead of respecting them? Have we made them caretakers, or have we set them free to be strong builders on firm foundations? Permission is hard to come by when we wait and wait for someone to tell us we have done well, that we have earned the right to be mature, respected adults. No, we give ourselves permission to grow, to live long and well, to prosper and be in good health.

I can tell my children that the way to get honor is to go to work and be good men and women.

CHIEF RUNNING BIRD

January 14

What we take for granted someone else thinks is beautiful. What we want to get rid of is someone else's treasure. Sometimes we stand so close to something dear that we cannot see that it is dear. Our lack of awareness robs us of what we assume is ours forever. We have many eyes, but most are closed or glazed over. The eyes of the mind and spirit perceive far more than our physical eyes will ever see. The eyes of our hearing detect sound but also feelings and attitude—and the music of the spheres. There is a word in the Cherokee language, *agowhtvhdi*, which means sight. When we touch something we not only feel but we also see the gentleness or the harshness, the depths and the heights. No, we are never blind except when we close ourselves off and deny the very Spirit of Life.

Give heed, my child, lift up your eyes, behold the One who has brought you life.

CEREMONIAL SONG

January 15

Feeling drained and weak in the knees is not so much a physical problem as an emotional one. Too much pressure drains away strength and we feel we are going to pieces. Inertia and lightheadedness may be the result of having to face something that seems beyond any power to overcome. But these will dissolve when met with strong words of strength and faith. As soon as strength takes hold and begins to flow again, we know we have struck down something so wily and subtle that it was both real and imaginary. But nothing has power against strong words, *"I will seek that which was lost, and bring again that which was driven away, and will bind up that which was broken, and will strengthen that which was sick."* And then we can ride the waves of our emotions like a canoe and not get upset among the waves.

Black Hawk is a true Indian, and disdains to cry like a woman.

BLACK HAWK

January 16

Rules are made to keep us safe and honest and well-organized—but many of them become more important than the purpose for which they were written. We have a tendency to make rules only to fall under the power of them. If rules and laws are made and have governed us for any length of time, it is generally thought that there can be no exceptions—even to the point of being ridiculous. When a rule becomes so binding that it will not allow common sense and honest action to help the people to do the right thing, it is time to make a change. Rules are made to help us do our best, or *i da tli ni gv si,* in Cherokee. Rules are made to serve human beings—not human beings made to serve the rules. We need the rules, but wisdom as well.

The Great Father in Washington says you have to go!
    INDIAN INSPECTOR, 1877

January 17

Most changes are too subtle to be noticed. The fog, *u gv ha dv*, that blankets the early morning, hangs so thick in the woods that the hills beyond cannot be seen. Then, without us seeing it, it is there no longer. So it is in our relationships with other people. We do not understand the moods and changes that work their silent influence on us when we least expect it. We react to the moods of others like we do to the fog, not realizing what has happened until the silent influence has gone. When our feelings are so in command, it is difficult to change the circumstances around us. All the experiences of a lifetime have influenced our decisions and made us react in a way that destroyed something that may never be rebuilt. When the fog lifts it takes away the veil so that we can see a long way. But the inner-fog hides life and love and friendship—until we change it.

I am satisfied . . . I am not afraid to avow the deed that I have done . . . I am willing to bury the toma-hawk and smoke the pipe of peace . . .

SOUWAHNOCK 1833

27

January 18

Acertain amount of protection from the wind makes it pleasant to walk in the deep woods, even in January—*Uno lv ta na*. It is quieter and without the activity of other seasons, but the deer come daily to feed on acorns that litter the moss-covered earth. Timing is important, even though the Cherokee has been said to have a time of his own—arriving and leaving as he sees fit. But even nature gets ahead of herself or lags behind at times. Here in the dead of winter, a shaft of sunlight brings out tiny moth-like insects that dance straight up and down, going nowhere. Doing the right thing at the right time is all-important. We tend to get overanxious and want to push ahead when it is not the time nor the right thing to do. We are not programmed by nature but by Spirit, and from that comes the wisdom to stay or act.

I beseech you . . . by everything you hold sacred and dear, abandon this wild visionary and desperate undertaking and return to your village.

KEOKUK 1832

January 19

We have to actively resist the suggestion that something is going to make us sick. It is not easy to talk illness and poverty without believing strongly that we may have to deal with them. The easiest way is to cancel negative suggestions and claim what we want. Money, which is *a de la* in Cherokee, will run for cover if we continually talk hardship—and we know what happens when someone tells us we do not look well. We begin to take our pulse and wonder whether we should lie down. Too much sympathy and self-pity destroys our immunity to difficulty. When we shut down on it and begin to talk health and begin to talk about excellent opportunities, then we open the way to be well and prosperous.

They came to you under the guise and pretense . . . and gained your confidence . . . they are enemies of you and your band, instead of friends.

KEOKUK 1832

January 20

When we rely on other people for what we need to know, we are vulnerable to their mistakes. What others give us may be sincere and it may be genuine, but all information is a matter of how we read it. What one person says with one meaning may reach the ear of another with a different understanding. Wisdom comes from the same source regardless of where we hear it, but it is better to take words of wisdom and work them through our own minds for direction and understanding. When someone else has answers that seem to apply to our questions, we can be open and teachable, but not gullible. It stands to reason if we tune our ears to answers within ourselves, we won't have to lean on outer sources for information.

The British father . . . promised aid and assistance . . . he is at peace with the Great Father in Washington . . . and neither knows nor cares for your grievances . . .

KEOKUK

January 21

In the darkest day in winter color is everywhere. They are colors we do not expect to see, so we do not see them. They float on early morning clouds that lie aloft in the southern sky and hover in the crevices of hills at midday. In the evening, the western horizon is purple—all shades of purple, which the Cherokee calls *gi ge s di*. The last rays of sunlight color the scudding clouds with purple, rose, and lilac. The Indian loves color and is tuned in to its joy. If we are caught in moods that are drab, our eyes have little chance of seeing color. A drab view can be changed. Even now a *sa go ni ge* (jay) and a brilliant *gi ga ge* (cardinal) can stir us with their blues and reds if we have the heart to see them.

This is the most valuable thing I have ever possessed.
YE-WHELL-COME-TETSA 1815

January 22

Pushmataha, Chief of the Choctaws, understood our weaknesses as well as our strengths. He knew how willing we are to give in to abuse for fear of having no peace at all. Peace at any price is very familiar to the American Indian. And we know how a little success can do away with common sense—how it can remove the stops that keep us on the true path. A stable attitude can offset the extremes where we sometimes find ourselves. Good peace — *to hi dv* — is an inside job, a place where we cultivate the development of our own spirits before we look to our surroundings for strength and sustenance. The heart and soul that loves peace and wants others to be peaceful will never miss the mark of excellence.

Never be elevated above measure by success . . . nor delighted with the sweets of peace to suffer insults.
PUSHMATAHA

January 23

As a child, I wanted to sing at the supper table. It seemed the logical place to let the joy of life flow freely—since it was our habit to share happy experiences at mealtime—never grievances. But *Eli si*, Grandmother Essie, expected manners, not singing. The food at our table was not as important as the stories. Some were farfetched yarns so typical of the Cherokee. When we came together, laughter and joyful bantering took my mind off the ever-present greens that I had to close my eyes to eat. Grandmother said greens were a part of making-do, but it seemed to me that I was making do when I sang at the table. Food should never be eaten when the throat is constricted and the spirit aches from hurt. Joy makes the most common food a feast—and it would not surprise me that *E li si* is sitting at supper in heaven—singing!

Friends and relations . . . you know what I feel . . . you have children, whom you love as yourself . . .

Wawatam 1763

33

January 24

Other people have no more power than we do. They may have the knack for making us think they can do anything. A little adjustment down in our minds will stop the thought that we must cope and compete with those who have greater advantages. If we believe anything holds us back, limits our ability, we can know beyond a doubt that more ability resides in us than we will ever have time to hone and develop. When we are doing something we love to do, it comes naturally to mind our own business and to polish our own skills. Love for the right work takes it out of the role of labor and competition and makes it into a work of art. Then, the little competitive self is dissolved into a powerful giant that didn't realize how much he was growing.

Your nation supposes that we, like the white people, cannot live without bread and pork and beer. But you ought to know that He, the Great Spirit and Master of Life has provided . . . for us in these spacious lakes . . . and woody mountains.

PONTIAC 1762

January 25

Giving up robs us of drawing up gold from our own depths. Imagine having a well, a very deep well, that is topped off with several feet of tainted water. But deeper down, the water, the *a ma'*, is clear, and down even farther it is a spring, a spring that bubbles cold and pure through deposits of gold. Should we give up because of what we saw in the beginning? Or would we want to tap the depths and clear away the polluted water and get down to the very best? If it is true that we only know five percent of who and what we are—then, it is possible that we have untapped depths, where our being is pure and free of contamination. Should we give up such a rich experience because of what we have seen on the surface?

We give you this belt to clear away all clouds, that we may live in bright sunshine . . .

HENDRICK 1754

January 26

There are in every life both sunshine people and rainy-day people. There are giving people and there are those who take, but how so few in number are those who understand. To have someone understand why we cry or laugh, why we feel downcast for no apparent reason, is to have a friend. A friend accepts our changes of mood without telling us to snap out of it. They know if we could so easily handle tears we would have done it already. All our loneliness and worry and fear seems to fade in the presence of a friend who never judges but stands alongside with loyalty. "My *u na li*, take my hand and walk with me until you can go alone." It gives us what we need to be a friend as well.

We shall not fail . . . to nourish your hearts . . . about the renewal of our amity and the brightening of the Chain of Friendship . . .

CANASSATEGO 1742

Habit has its beginning in thought. Whatever becomes second nature to us has first caught on in our thinking—only to operate, in time, without thinking at all. Breaking with deeply ingrained addictions is something else again. Since we were old enough to understand we have been bent to a certain thought, molded to act and react until we follow through habitually. If what we did gave us comfort or made us feel good, we did it again. We have to fight habit with habit, deliberately changing one thought, one action, for another. If we simply try to remove a habit without filling the vacuum, we are opening the door for more and worse to come in. It is harder when we let thought drift back to remember how we were comforted. There is more than one comfort, more than one joy in forming a new habit.

We bury them from sight forever and plant again the Tree.

DEKANAWIDAH 1720

January 28

Speak to me of serenity, of treasures yet to be found, of peace that flows like a river. Tell me of tranquil places that no hand has marred, no storm has scarred. Give me visions of standing in sunlight or the feeling of spring mist against my cheek as I live and move and breathe. Show me paths that wind through wild lilies and beds of buttercups. Sing me songs like the mingled voices of wrens and meadowlarks, the lowing of gentle cows, the soft mother-call of a mare to her colt. Lead me past a glass-smooth pond where frogs croak of coming-out parties, their graduation from frisky tadpoles to squat green frogs. Find me a place in the sunlight to sit and think and listen to the sweet inner voice that says so quietly, "Peace, be still."

To hi ge se s di
    PEACE ON EARTH.

January 29

New life comes in only as we turn loose of the old. There must be a place for what we want or need. If there is not a place prepared, the new circumstances flow on by—and we are left with the same things we have always had. If we think we cannot bear to part with an old way of life, we are not ready to accept anything new. Instead we can make a personal decision, a firm commitment, to forget what is behind and push forward to what is ahead. Our mental and spiritual attitudes make room for new life when we set them in motion with our words. Nothing will overtake us, not love, not prosperity, not peace and joy— until we make a place for them and ask them to come in. Hope, alone, does not do it, but a firm decision for a new life will clear the way.

My people, before the white man came you were happy. You had many buffalo to eat and tall grass for your ponies—you could come and go like the wind.
    Wovoka

January 30

Waiting tests our grit and faith, and anything else we have on the line. We activate every nerve in us to move, to do something—and then we wait. But if we wait a little longer with patience and endurance, we will know what to do. During this period, we can stir up the gifts that are in us, encourage ourselves to be strong and calm, to find a calm center in the midst of all the whirling debris around us. When we can wait with *u li he li s di* (joy), it connects us to the right things, puts us in the right place to receive. Joy is not of the emotions but of the spirit, and it can bubble up and grow in our weakest moments.

We have learned that though there are many papers in Washington upon which are written promises to pay us for our lands, no white man seems to remember them.

FOUR GUNS

Sensible people do not get ruffled easily and are known to be reliable in a crisis. We want these stable people with us as friends and team members when the game is terribly important. We have heard the calm voice and felt the strong hand when our knees wobbled and our hands shook. It is easy to recall those who sustained us with their words, their caring. And sadly, we remember those who did not. Whatever common sense is, the heart has it, not the head. It is having the right priorities, knowing what is important, and giving as much as, or more than, we have received. Indians of old had this stalwart strength to stand like straight arrows to give support. They reached out to lift someone before they stopped to think whether he deserved it. The price is the same now as then—patience, love, loyalty—those things that seem so scarce.

I learned many English words . . . could recite some of the Ten Commandments . . . I knew how to sleep in a bed, pray to Jesus, comb my hair, use a toilet . . . I learned that a person thinks with his head instead of his heart.

Sun Chief 1890

FEBRUARY

Gaga lu'nee
Bony or Hungry Month

The whole earth belongs to
ASGA YA GALUN LATI, *the Great
Spirit.*

CHEROKEE PEOPLE

February 1

This morning the sun spilled pale gold over the horizon and filled all the space beneath the great oaks. High above, the red-tail hawk, known to the Cherokees as *ta wo di,* sailed lazily along air currents. Even though spring is still many weeks away, the land is beautiful to see. Now, while the trees are bare, there is a wider view of hills and valleys. The colors are all muted shades of beige and gray and the hills are swathed in blue mist. Even the deer are outfitted by nature to be the same subtle shade of browns and tans to give them protection. A restful moment is a perfect moment. But we have to be open to it, and receptive to anything that gives us peace of mind with no side effects. It can't happen if our minds are set to be drab and dreary.

The old Lakota was wise. He knew that man's heart away from nature becomes hard.
STANDING BEAR

February 2

The drawback of having something go wrong is that we start believing we can't do anything right. It is the beginning of a habit that makes us stumble where we have always stumbled. A subtle and secret conditioning sets in to make us believe we will fail—even before we start. It makes us wilt at the first sign of opposition, devastating us with criticism. It is then that we lose our grip and our good intentions—not just for the present time but for all time to come. The Cherokee learned long ago to say, "We no longer fall down when something challenges us. We no longer see ourselves as victims. But we are strong and able to overcome the most severe critic and break every habit that has kept us bound."

Each day in the old times in summer and in winter, we came down to the river to bathe. This strengthened and toughened our firm skin.

CHIPAROPAI

February 3

These are no longer ordinary times, and many circumstances we thought would never change, are changing. The innocent times, the good natured humor of life has been covered over with suggestive jokes empty of meaning. The ground is shifting under our feet and we are having to learn to walk a new way. Few things are permanent. We are born of change, but we still have to keep a commonsense attitude or we can lose our footing. We need to prove, long before we accept something as fact, that it is true. If it is right, it can be proved. Much is a mystery to us. But to the *Tsilagi* — Cherokee — silence is golden. We speak little and listen long. Words are important in songs and in ceremonies—and in general conversation as well. It is wise to save words and use them only when they can be effective.

Good words do not last long until they amount to something.
CHIEF JOSEPH

February 4

To stand alone does not mean there is no one else around. It means we are *u na tse li dv-u na to tiv hi*...we think for ourselves in an independent way, using our heads rather than our feet. We fit life to us instead of letting it press us into a mold that would not make us happy. Letting the world dictate to us is being one of the herd that runs—not because it is the right thing to do, but because we think everyone else is doing it, and so must we. Is it the right direction? Refusing to be swept along with every trend is cultivating our inner awareness of right and wrong. Awareness is there within us, but we have to hear it and heed it. This is why we were given intelligence—to stand alone so that we may have something to offer when someone else needs us.

Too many misinterpretations have been made . . . too many misunderstandings . . .

CHIEF JOSEPH

February 5

If we could look ahead, we would be comforted to know that what we have worked for and what we have given our hearts to will reward us. We cannot give and give and not receive, especially if we have given willingly and cheerfully. Our lives are many-faceted. We have shared in many ways and many times when it seemed unimportant. We gave without thought that it would do anything but help— and these are the gifts that will not go unrewarded. Giving is so often thought of in terms of the things we give, but our greatest giving is of our time, and kindness, and even comfort for those who need it. We look on these gifts as unimportant—until we need them. Then, the most wonderful gift is simple courage.

I felt that I was leaving all that I had, but I did not cry.

WETATONMI, 1877

February 6

Little things heal our hurts. Sounds, scents, the spoken word, and music that may mean nothing to someone else can reach into our souls and do a work that ordinary methods cannot touch. Simple remedies can heal the deepest ills—a love that springs from inner wells, the sounds of birdsong and the laughter of children at play. Our work is to avoid the negative side—to think and speak only healing words, loving words. Choices are possible. Though we make many of them a day, we do it so unconsciously that we have not realized their effect—fretting about every little thing, letting the world steal our peace, and lying down when we should be up and doing. Choose to be well, to find contentment and to be a role model for those who watch. Listen for peace.

Listen! Or your tongue will make you deaf.
    CHEROKEE SAYING

February 7

Always remember that certain circumstances are not ours to alter. We make the most of them and go on. We can only be examples, never controllers of other people's lives, other people's children, other people's circumstances. Some would have us believe we contribute to harsh events by doing nothing. But some of the best work, some of the deepest caring and doing is not physically evident in the beginning. Help of any kind must be wanted and recognized before it can do any good. Too much help where it is not appreciated can make even a good person helpless. We have to be wise in our giving, and particularly wise in what we withhold, because it may be what we withhold helps the most.

We were contented to let things remain as the Great Spirit made them.

CHIEF JOSEPH, 1873

February 8

I t is interesting to see someone take one little idea and make it grow into something that benefits many people. Could it be that an idea hangs before us like a worm in a chrysalis that is able to emerge as a beautiful *ka ma ma*—butterfly? When we reach for the stars we should remember that we are rooted and grounded in little things. The basis for success that lasts is the knowledge that slow and careful construction cannot be toppled by fickle and fast-moving tastes. So much is made to be temporary—the fast-moving fads—and people jump aboard to ride them for the duration. In the process the *ka ma ma* is crushed before it ever develops, and the pupa-idea must begin all over again. But it remembers its beginnings, its basic purpose.

I may be forced to adopt a new way of life, but my heart and spirit spring from the red earth.
PAINTED WOLF

February 9

To some, power is domination, ruling anything defenseless. But that isn't power, it is abuse, and abuse is cowardly. Abuse takes advantage where it can, always pretending to be the victim, but looking for the opportunity to overpower. Forget the idea that power is from the world. Whole worlds have been changed in minutes. Power that was bold and bragging can suddenly be a whimper. Empires have crashed and those that caused so much misery have deflated like balloons. Real power is not *nigvnhdiha*, which is understood by the Cherokee to be *put on*. It is from an inner source, characteristically calm, like a great river that flows smoothly but drives huge cities with energy. A single drop of water seems powerless and takes the way of least resistance, but joined to all the others, it has force. One person may seem inadequate to change anything, but united with others, can change anything.

The red man must leave the land of his youth and find a new home in the far west.
SHABONEE 1827

February 10

Turn around right where you are and face the frightening situation, the lion, *hlvdaji,* on your path. Don't waver and dodge. Look the problem in the eye and call it nothing. Speak to it in definitive words so that there is no doubt that it must go. Wisdom tells us to get out of harm's way at times, but it never tells us to weep with fear. Once we turn to face it, a quiet determined strength pours in to end the terror. Fear is terrorism. It is not running from it that cripples us but refusing to call it what it is. When fear takes over it flows through all our thinking. If we have any faith at all, it is scared faith, but faith will grow when we charge it with determination and powerful words.

Make everything straight and strong.
    DRAGGING-CANOE

February 11

Many things from the past echo faintly within us—voices, sounds, thoughts. Only a few ring clear like a bell from many long ago seasons. Persistent memories call us back to deal with details—some of them best forgotten. Why do we remember? Perhaps to clarify what we feel, to help us be more objective about the present moment. Or maybe to force us to see the pattern of our own lives so that we may throw out events that have been obstacles. Sometimes we remember just so we can be grateful. Like the well-fed dog that turns primitive at the sight of a bone, we pick up on our own instincts and react before we think. If we see what is about to happen we can meet it with good humor and have less need to make everyone in the present time pay dearly for what happened so long ago.

I want peace, that we may . . . sleep in our houses and rise in peace on both sides.
    BLOODY-FELLOW

February 12

The Cherokee can agree with Sir Francis Drake when he wrote about the herb garden, "A perfect garden planted with herbs, when trod upon gives the very air a delightful fragrance." But to the Cherokee it meant even more—food and medicine. As a child, I spent much time following my Grandmother Essie in search of herbs, mullein, lamb's quarter and other things I hoped I wouldn't have to eat in greens, but the hunt was a joy. Kneeling to dig the herbs, feeling the soil and the warmth of the sun, gave me the realization that the plants were only a part of a gift from *Asga Ya Galun lati*. I was also being given the day to day enjoyment, the songs of dozens of birds, the little meal I shared with Grandmother, and her company away from others.

A Cherokee woman is never idle and has no time to tattle or to create mischief.
WILLIAM FYFFE

February 13

Once a person gets despair out of the way, few things can slow his progress. Despair is the dividing line between those who can take impossibility in stride and those who wilt at the first sign of opposition. Too much energy is absorbed in despair. Strength gives way to weakness and weakness robs us of the will to overcome. Anything that wastes energy should be left behind. Energy cuts doubt to the bone. When a word of power is spoken, new strength is generated. Power words are not just *u wo du hi*, pretty words, but strong words of courage that are heard in the ear and then in the heart where they stay to do a perfect work.

This is a serious time with you. May the Lord bring you out of all your troubles. Trust your course with Him.

CHIEF JOHN ROSS

February 14

Our wounds need time to heal. And when it seems the healing has done its work, protection from further hurt is necessary, because our scars are on the surface. Physical wounds are bad enough, but when they come from mental cruelty and unfair treatment, pain returns again and again to reopen what no one should have to bear. It seems almost a sacrilege to ask someone so deeply hurt to forgive those who caused it. Yet unforgiveness causes damage almost as devastating as physical wounds, or more so. There is great stress in bearing grudges and the abused do not need any new pain or new problems. Forgiveness does not set the abusive free, but the abused.

I was living peaceably and satisfied when people began to speak bad of me.

GERONIMO

February 15

Once change begins it often comes in multiples, ranging from easily handled small changes to the great ones that can become unwieldy. When this is the case, it tends to scatter our forces. It is harder to achieve order and staying power when our attention is scattered. There is a calm center to everything. Even a tornado, which the Cherokee calls *u no le,* swirls around a calm eye. Most calm places are very small, but small cells of tranquillity can be the seed of greater peace. We have to believe in peace—even though we cannot always feel it. It is within us and it will grow if we give it the opportunity. With peace of mind, doors open, the tide turns, and something good breaks for us. It is good enough reason to work toward solutions rather than dwelling on problems.

Stand fast and remain united and all will soon be well.

Chief John Ross

February 16

The biggest mountain is made up of tiny grains of sand and earth. The swiftest, widest river is only tiny drops of water. And in the swell of the human race, you are just as important as the next person. It helps to know that one little drop of water is as complete in itself as the whole river or the entire sea. Even in the smallest way, a person is just as complete and miraculous as any smart invention on earth. It is only by words and actions that circumstances differ and lives take different routes. Each tiny part of anything is infinitely important. Each petal on a daisy is necessary to give it balance to stand straight on its stem. Never say you are not important. You are not just important, you are essential. You have a definite purpose and it is a sacred responsibility.

We have reason to glory in the achievements of our ancestors.

O no'sa

February 17

Touching the earth is a lovely thing, a feeling of once again finding our beginnings, a knowing that this place where we stand, whether to walk or plow or plant, is something created for us, for the pulse of the earth slows our own and tranquilizes our confusion. The Cherokees believe that seeing the sky in all its limitless depths stirs our imaginations and stretches our awareness of how much simple beauty is provided for us. We can see that bitterness lasts only as long as we allow it, but we have reached beyond the ceiling of our minds and are as unlimited as the sky. As currents of air stir the fragrance of flowers, we may not be able to see all things but we sense the influence and know that life is ours to enjoy. It comes by Divine heritage.

Ka wat lee os, tat gat eh'. Peace for the Cherokees, Oh, America, peace for the Cherokees.

February 18

We need to get our priorities in a row. A lazy person never has priorities and never plans anything. He lets circumstances make all his decisions—and believes fate has the final say. Even though he has had a thousand nudges to do a certain thing, he ignores them because it is only himself dreaming again. If we cannot hold onto a plan long enough to do anything about it, then we should write it. Write it so plain that when we read it, we run—we run toward putting into practice what we set out on paper. It is essential to decide the ultimate outcome of our lives. If we do nothing, then that is a decision. Our lot in life is what we make it, using every delay, every pain, every injustice as fuel to fire our determination.

Let the young men of this nation remember that idleness leads to poverty. Industry is honorable and leads to contentment.

CHIEF JOHN ROSS

February 19

Wе all discover at some time or other that it is painful to love. Caring about something, about someone, about some place is a great joy. It does make us vulnerable, easy to get to, easy to touch, and hard-pressed to hide our emotions. Some bit of us wants desperately to hide what we feel for fear that it will be taken the wrong way. But even more, we are afraid of revealing more than we are willing to share. A reserve of our own thoughts and feelings keeps us from depleting all that we are, keeps us from giving away that part of us which generates life. It keeps us able to love and care deeply. Despite all the pain that goes with caring, we would not have it any other way.

The earth has received the embrace of the sun and we shall see the results of that love.
    SITTING BULL

February 20

We are tempted at every turn to give in to things that are not good for us. Numerous tangible things and acts run through our minds to delight and lure us away from our good intentions, but none as powerful as that first thought, that subtle invitation to give in. It is always the first step, the first word, the first taste that leads us like the pipes of Pan. We innocently muse that we have been really good lately, keeping our schedules, doing what we think is important. Isn't it time we rewarded ourselves? Why not indulge a little—just this once? These are the first of a series of questions. Later comes the sad question—what did I do to deserve this? This is the place to stop saying how stupid we are, get back in the boat, and start paddling as fast as we can—even if it is upstream!

Youth is impulsive. When our young men grow angry at some real or imaginary wrong . . . it denotes their hearts are black . . .
　　SEATTLE

February 21

A young Indian boy named Slow was so brave in battle when he was fourteen that he was renamed Sitting Bull. He had a great love for birds and imitated their songs—finally writing songs of his own and chanting them. How many of us have been called slow? If not in one category, then in another. The change comes when we study something we love, doing what comes so naturally that we succeed in an area that was totally unexpected. Never underestimate the power of small beginnings. Sufficiency in all things more often than not begins in small ways. Little ideas and tiny steps evolve into greater accomplishment. Someone said it takes twenty years to become an overnight success, but it only takes seconds to recognize the beginning of one.

Let us look forward to the pleasing landscape of the future.

CHIEF ROSS

February 22

We are persons with a desire for variety. Rigid routine can make our spirits sag. Following the same path at the same time every day, repeating and repeating without the slightest change, dulls the spirit. Life gets to be routine because we let our minds fall into a rut that has no future. Nagging fear enters when living falls into inertia, and we are troubled not so much by what is going on around us as what is going on inside. There are many words for spirit, but the Cherokees call it *a da nv to*, or life, *v le ni to nv*. It means to show some initiative, some serious intention. It is not something we only hope to have one day. It is a necessity—moisture that feeds the roots and sunlight that draws new life. But it must be stirred up.

Warriors stir up themselves to go to battle—and so must we.

STRONG LEGS

February 23

A winner carries with him the quiet knowledge that he has heard every argument, faced every opposition, felt every criticism, but there is no turning back and no accepting defeat. Rejection is one of the oldest forms of torture. If a dozen people approve of us and one does not, our thought is riveted on the one and what his reason is for not liking us. But time and circumstances change so swiftly. Nothing stays the same. What was real and possible is suddenly out of reach or we find amazing success where we have failed a dozen times. If we give up, we forfeit everything. Look beyond rejection, see beyond limits, think around the bend in the road. It may be that we have been trying to settle for less than the best—and we have been doing it for a long time.

The path of glory is rough and many gloomy hours obscure it. May the Great Spirit shed light on yours.
    BLACK HAWK 1833

February 24

Worthy performances do not make us who we are, but little things and what we tell ourselves in the privacy of our own minds. We are what we see and what we believe is important. We are children to the end—innocent in ways we do not understand, aware of our spiritual connections and afraid to develop them. What would people think? How will I explain that I no longer enter into those activities that are thought so clever? There's a world of things we do not have to explain. As much as we want others to understand and like us, if it takes us off our standing place into a world of unlikely places, then we flirt with disaster. No one can dictate to us if we are not listening. We will not lose our footing if we are not teetering. We are who we are by what we choose to cultivate, and all worthy performances are made up of very little parts.

God made me an Indian.
    SITTING BULL 1876

February 25

When we stop fretting we gain more ground. If we can stop trying to control everything with our minds and let it go, even for a little while, we will get a clearer view. There is wisdom in the words, "Having done all, stand." Do what can be done, build faith, know there is a Great Holy Spirit that knows even the very smallest thing we need. At this point, everything will challenge us, but just let it slide away, let it dissolve from inattention. The greatest steps are taken when we decide not to thrash out, not to hate and resent and lose ourselves in the confusion. Put it all down and walk away to something totally different. Having done all, stand, and refuse to be drawn back into a place of no peace.

The man who sat on the ground in his tipi meditating on life and its meaning, accepting the kinship of all creatures and acknowledging unity with the universe of things, was infusing into his being the true essence of civilization.

CHIEF LUTHER STANDING BEAR

February 26

Most of us are like the trees that grow along the moist ravine. We are where we get the best nourishment. Others are undernourished and don't know what to do about it. Many times they reject the very thing that would help because of their preconceived notion and misunderstanding of what is true. Obviously, if what we are doing shows no improvement in us, we are not doing the right thing. Most answers and remedies are simple if we were not so hardheaded and determined to make it complicated. The sooner we recognize emotions, lack of rest, and a constant flow of negative thought as enemies, the sooner we get a handle on the real problem. It takes constant monitoring to know ourselves as we really are and begin to clear the way.

One old elm under which the representatives of the tribes were wont to meet — will cover us all.

WA-O-WO-WA-NO-ONK 1847

February 27

"It is important to have a vision that is not clouded with fear," said a Cherokee leader. "As children we were able to see beyond the impossible by enjoying a vision of how we wanted things to be. It required unlimited joy, and life responded freely— until we grew up enough that everything had to be real." Sometimes the vision is truer than that which comes from it. A pattern to make anything can be accurate, and if followed perfectly, can produce the perfect model of it. But bringing something forth is the problem. We have to have a steady hand and a mind that is willing to follow precisely. Few things are spelled out for us. We learn to focus on what we need, but there is still another step: Focus on fulfillment. See it completed. This is usually left out as we adopt a wait-and-see attitude, and this step is far too important to ignore.

Have a vision not clouded by fear.
THE CHEROKEE

February 28

Memories are simply patterns stamped on our minds. Don't let them make you believe you have done everything wrong. Make new choices, find new thoughts that feed your spirit. Speak courage. Intentionally cut sorrow and regret from your thought. Get rid of tears and, if you have to, force yourself to begin smiling. It is not ridiculous to set new standards. It is common sense to turn your life around when it doesn't work the way it is. Forget what others say and believe in the Good Father. It is their privilege to make decisions about their lives, but it is up to you to make your own. We are saying the same thing, we just say it in a different way. Find your own path and fill it with flowers. See something beautiful everywhere you look. Rejoice in life itself and find your own new and happier road.

There is one God looking down on us all. We are all children of one God. God is listening to me. The sun, the darkness, the winds, are all listening to what we now say.

GERONIMO

MARCH

Unu 'la hee"
Windy Month

We the great mass of the people think only of the love we have for our land, for we do love the land where we were brought up.

CHIEF JOHN ROSS

March 1

We thought they would last forever—those old ones who taught us, bent us, sweetened our lives. We thought our questions would always go to them, and answers would return in familiar voices. Too many times we did not appreciate their humor, their words that chided us with lessons. Our differences were great, we thought. Our eyes wandered to other things, our voices mingled with strange ones. And suddenly, like the vapor mists that lift and fade on sun-struck mountain tops, they were gone. We did not see them go. They slipped past the boundaries to joy and rest without limit. Now the questions hang in mid-air without voices to answer. And the differences fade like the mists but memory persists with genuine humor, genuine love, and we, in turn, convince our young to, "Hear me now, my children . . ."

I have dreamed that he shall live to count many coups and be old.

GRANDFATHER OF PLENTY-COUPS 1848

March 2

"I have a right!" Only, says a wise sage, if you accept the responsibility that goes with it. We have a right to be full-fledged people of dignity and decency and respect, as long as we are decent and respectful to those around us. The right for a good life belongs to all of us—as long as we value it, work for it, and keep it good. We have a right to speak our minds, but we have to know the tremendous responsibility of words. We have a right to cultivate our spiritual preferences and to see them bear fruit in every good thing. It is our right to be who we are without the burden of regret and resentment. But we have to remember that our rights are limited to where our rights end—and another person's rights begin.

These were not our ways. We kept the laws we made and lived our religion. We have never been able to understand the white man, who fools nobody but himself.

PLENTY COUPS 1848

March 3

A great man once said that a human soul may be thought of as seeking a creative outlet. If that outlet is clear and free, all is well. But if the channel is clogged with fuss and worry, we can forget the creativity. Even in quiet, we can be in a frenzy. Quiet desperation, Thoreau called it. True silence comes from directing thought to quiet places and still waters. If we allow our minds to drift toward something that could go wrong, then it steals our peace and clogs our creative capacity. Sit quietly and think of softly flowing water, gentle breezes, and the call of the whippoorwill. Reflect on the joy of thinking freely, of unlimited vitality—and don't tell yourself that it couldn't possibly happen.

The American Indian is skilfully artistic, a refined sense that springs from deep wells of ancient vision.
MURPHY

March 4

Few things that count in life are taken by great strides. Little by little, step by step, we inch forward. Great progress in a short time is so often short-lived and gives us the wrong idea of how things work. We build a consciousness, use good judgment, *di gu go ta nv* in Cherokee, to move slowly and with awareness. But as we build, it is important to override the negatives that try to lodge in what we are doing. Our thinking is like a garden that needs to be cultivated. And our talking is even more important. The two go *i tsu la*, hand in hand, and what happens is a direct result of what we have dwelled on for many seasons. But it is in our power to make corrections and edge out trouble—little by little, but very surely.

Certain small ways and observances sometimes have connection with large and more profound ideas.

STANDING BEAR

March 5

It is sad when our children have not been able to rely on us to build their self-esteem. The Cherokees call it *qa lv quo di*. Even those of us that have come a long way have memories that need a loving touch. Parents teach only what they know to teach. But we are not set forever in one direction. We reach an age when we must teach ourselves. We learn to forgive and to understand that when we get to the fork in the road we will know the right way. Why go the wrong way because someone before us did? If our self-esteem has been damaged, feeding it more pity and more ill-treatment is not healing it. Criticism is passed to us the same way blue eyes and dark hair are inherited. But criticism can be changed and replaced with love. This is a decision that changes our lives—and those who follow as well.

Civilized people depend too much on man-made printed pages. I turn to the Great Spirit's book which is the whole of his creation.

TATANGA MANI

March 6

Remember when you do anything, there will be someone that will find fault, no matter what you do. The pleasure of an unhappy person is to find something wrong in others to salve his own discontent. The Cherokees believe that tests sharpen their wit and help them *a s qua dv*, win or triumph over opposite powers. It would be beneath them to accept criticism as something they must overcome. The Cherokees flick it off like *to si*, pesky mosquitos. We all try to understand our differences of opinion, to care what effect we cause in other people. But the bane of anyone's existence is ignorance—our own. We want more than anything to correct what we know is wrong. And what we find wrong in others may be a reflection of our own wrongs.

May the white man and the Indian speak truth to each other today.

BLACKFOOT

March 7

The first thing in the morning when our feet touch the floor, our feelings begin to feed us impressions. Not only do they review our situation in a few seconds, they decide if this is a good day or if it should be one of anxiety. This is the precise time to hush feelings and paint the day the way we want it to be—not to be fed from the negative side. We tell the wrong impressions that they are not acceptable, that we feel different than we have in the past. This is a new day and we are free and happy, able to change what needs to be changed, to do what needs to be done. There are times when we must go against our own feelings and dictate what we will have, shaping and reshaping the hours as we see fit.

When I make peace, it is a long and lasting one. There is no end to it.
SANTANA

March 8

Nature has her indecisive moments. *A ma ga nu go gv,* the season when new life springs up, may come early with its wildflowers and blossoming trees. She is known for her adolescent behavior, all smiles and flowers in her hair, only to be in tears in a few minutes. We think, this is it, we will never change our opinion. No, we will not be moved, we will cling to this one idea and time cannot erode any part of it. There can be no parting with this idea, nothing and no one can make us think differently. Spring may hint that she is here—so we can relax. But she is never adamant that she will not change. It is only the human being that claims such powers. But the power that keeps us moving and changing and becoming better is not our power but *Galun lati.*

We will never let our hold to this land go for we say to you that our father who sits in heaven gave it to us.
AITOOWEYAH, THE STUD, AND KNOCK DOWN

March 9

We are not always granted the privilege of going back and doing things differently. If we were, could we? We might if we had new knowledge. Otherwise, we would do the same thing we did before. It was all we knew. Every race has had its Trail of Tears, in fact, every individual has suffered and agonized over what he might have done. Gentle people hope that by cooperation things will work for all concerned. It isn't in the hearts of the gentle to think that others do not have their same heart-felt ways. But challenges in the present time are sufficient without adding the past. If we know so much now, we need to use it. We can, sometimes, project ahead by looking back objectively to tap some reserve of knowledge. If we lack such inner knowledge, if we lack wisdom, we need to ask. And then we listen for the still small voice of direction.

Chief Ross led in prayer and when the bugle sounded and the wagons started rolling many of the children waved their little hands goodbye to their mountain homes.

PRIVATE JOHN BURNETT

March 10

The more stress we have the less we like other people—and ourselves. A little pressure is sufficient. Stress can be productive if it is something we like doing. But when we can no longer *ka no gi a*, enjoy and sing about life, we need to re-evaluate the direction we are going. It is impossible to withdraw from every problem, but neither can we go on without some relief. Being responsible is a natural part of life—very necessary to living well and being contented. To find a happy medium is to center ourselves where peace and answers can be found. It does not come from the noise and complaints of the world—but from that secret place of harmony and strength within the heart. It is a place that must be added to and kept harmonious, for it gives us poise and renewal when we need it.

Once you have heard the meadowlark and caught the scent of fresh-plowed earth, peace cannot escape you.

SEQUICHIE

March 11

Can you see the wind? Can you see the fragrance of flowers floating on the breezes? Can you see thought or what it is that changes a tree from bare limbs and brown leaves to lush green? Can you see love or joy or peace? We can only see evidence of these invisible things, and it is enough to make us know they do exist. The substance of life is so evident, so real and beautiful. Why is it that we ever question the existence of our Creator, who set all things in motion? Are we so base, so grounded that unless it gives us momentary pleasure, feeds our starving appetites, we cannot recognize the greatest help available? It is *Galun lati*, the Great Holy Spirit, invisible but more real than all we see that is tangible.

We see the changes of day and night . . . the seasons, the stars, the moon, the sun. Anyone must know it is the work of some one more powerful than man.

CHASED-BY-BEARS

March 12

It is too easy to believe we are at the end of the line when it is only the beginning. One more step, one more effort may be all that is needed. It would amaze us if we knew how close we are to stepping past an old barrier—and it would shake us to know how close we came to quitting. Some would say it is too late—that too much has happened, we cannot go back and recapture what was lost. We have destroyed too much, bent the twig too far. And so it is true in some things. It is true that we have hurt and been hurt. We can't go back, but the spiritual basis on which we stand can lift us up. Sometimes we have to sift our own lives to see what is worth saving, and then we find the Great Spirit made us. What He made is good and we should not let it go to waste. It is the time to turn over a new leaf to rediscover Divine connections.

Martin Luther King said, "I have a dream." But we Indians didn't have a dream. We had a reality.

BEN BLACK ELK

March 13

There are special places in our lives that live on forever. Just entering there in memory makes them live again. We feel the heat and the cold, catch the fragrance so familiar, the aroma of certain foods, or even hear a bit of a song. There are too many reasons to count, too many feelings, for us ever to lose touch with some part of us that was then—and is now. People are part of our memories, too—living within our thoughts and influencing our thinking like the wind that we feel but cannot see. We are made up of many things, many experiences that we do not want to lose, but we also have the power to keep yesterday in its place and make the most of today. Yesterday was the foundation, but today is the house, and we're living there and keeping things in their proper order.

As a child I understood how to give; I have forgotten this grace since I became civilized.

OHIYESA

87

March 14

Few things can dominate nature when she is about to make a change. Relentless and determined, she has a plan and it may take a few runs before the door is slammed on winter—but it is coming quickly. A subtle greening has begun in sheltered places. The wild rose canes laid flat by cold winter winds are no longer gray. Purple striped dayflowers and tiny four-petal blue-eyes bloom profusely with a minimum of sunlight and warm air. The wild strawberry known to Cherokees as *a ni,* has put out new leaves, and we see the eternal miracle that never grows old—the new baby calf. When frost put down the flowers and stopped the birds from singing last fall, spring seemed far away. Now she is knocking on the door, and if we answer her with seeds she will hide again. But not for long. We just need a little time to prepare. If we are to see it all, we must begin now.

We were content to let things remain as the Great Spirit has made them.
CHIEF JOSEPH

March 15

Why judge yourself by what someone else is saying? They only know what they think. Can we fit our lives into the narrow confines of theirs? We can search our own souls. And most likely, we will find that we have connections uniquely our own—deeper in many ways than those with whom we would like to be in accord. But there's no way we can whip ourselves into being like someone else. We can only make ourselves better. Regardless of how we have been conditioned to think, we know right from wrong. It is innate and speaks loud enough that if we want to hear it, we will. The only thing that keeps us from hearing is the clamor of voices outside ourselves—and they have no other purpose but to destroy. Don't dally with trouble. Refuse to be a part of anything you would not look at in the light.

Each man is good in His sight. It is not necessary for eagles to be crows.
SITTING BULL

March 16

It seems there is often too much of one thing and not enough of the other. Balance has a way of disappearing when we need it most. But it is our fault for thinking that once we have things all working together it will stay in balance without our having to do anything else. Nothing is so set that it will never change. We should never give in to challenges that throw us off center. Wait a little while. Something may be working that we don't know about. Don't accept everything as it appears. It can change in a moment's notice and swing our way. Very often the law of nonresistance is at work here. Some of our best decisions are based on standing still until we can get a true picture.

When life is easy, complex patterns of life can develop.
COOWEESCOOWEE

March 17

Remembering is painful at times. It is so easy to relive what happened, and what did not happen, and we try to take all the blame. A fortunate few can look back and delight in the memory of times past. Most see it as a reflection of our own guilt. We know what guilt is. Why did we not do a better job, pay more attention, follow a hunch? It is probably because we are better at hindsight than we will ever be in seeing things as they are now. Would we have done differently if we knew then what we know now? Maybe. But how could we see past the bend in the road? The best thing we can do for ourselves is to forgive. Forgiving heals. It clears the way for quality time—time to build and love, and renew and restore. It is what the Cherokees call *a da to li s di*, a time of grace when we have done nothing to deserve it.

I am tired of fighting . . . from where the sun now stands, I will fight no more.
  CHIEF JOSEPH

March 18

Other people have so much happen in their lives before we get to know them that we don't always know how to meet their needs. If they have been hurt they may box themselves in and our reach is not long enough. But we cannot go back and make up for what someone else has done. All of us have come to the present with some memory, some experience, that has affected us negatively. It would be hard to live in a world of hurt and not be touched by it. But the Cherokee knows that change can take place suddenly to heal life. A Seneca chief had been sick a long time, but he was visited in his dreams by three supernatural beings sent by the Great Spirit, and rose up cured to teach the good message given him by the Master of Life. His people thrived and flourished and developed gifts. So can we. When we seek we find. And it may be by helping others.

We were a lawless people, but we were on pretty good terms with the Great Spirit.
  WALKING BUFFALO

March 19

Last autumn's leaves have been dislodged from their wintering places to race north with the wind from the south—only to be turned and blown south again. They drift and dance on end, twirling and falling into deep piles to disintegrate in spring rains. Drifting with the wind is not a habit of nature alone. People with no goals, no aims, drift from one place to another in hopes that fate will put them in the right place at the right time. Fate is simply accepting what comes because nothing has been done to direct thought and action in any other way. If decisions are not made and goals are not set, the world will make them for us. The Cherokee calls this attitude *go na ya*, which translates to the same thing as "doing without."

The problem with blending the Indian and European cultures is that the Indian is devoted to living and the European to getting.
JOHN ROSS MCINTOSH

March 20

Someone said the test of courage is not to give up but to rise up and take dominion over melancholy moods. To give in to mood swings from sadness to anger makes finding stable ground even more difficult. In fact, it probably causes more *nu ne lv na,* which in Cherokee means mischief or harm, than any other thing. When talking to someone trustworthy does not ease the stress, then writing it can make a world of difference. Writing it to ourselves can bring out many causes for sadness or anger that we didn't know we were harboring. A daily journal has been the source of help in learning what we store away unconsciously, only to come out and whip us at the most unlikely times. It is a way of cleaning house and making corrections in the privacy of our own minds without having to tell the world.

Do not hurt your neighbor, for it is not him you wrong but yourself.
    THE SHAWNEE

March 21

Other people have problems the same way we do. If they get loud about them, we don't have to react. Resistance makes difficult times even more difficult to handle. It helps not to threaten but to let things cool down naturally. The Cherokee word for this is *to hi ge se s di,* making peace, or peace for the earth. Forgiveness seems to be a necessity for so many things that are wrong. Forgiveness never degrades but elevates, and is not to let someone else get away with something but to free ourselves from an entanglement. It frees us from bitter resentment that can make us sick—and can help heal the sickness if it is already there. Eventually, it makes us glad that we did not react, doing and saying things for which we would later be sorry.

They fight among themselve, but if you strike at them they will turn on you.
LITTLE CROW 1951

March 22

Everything in the world cannot be judged by one mistake. When we have fallen short or someone seems to have failed us, we can leave it there where it happened. There is no use in stirring old trouble into every new thing we do. There are things that seem to break our hearts; pain that goes on and on. But we can work through. If we are strong and don't let our hands grow weak and slack, our work will be rewarded. We grieve for the loss of things, or persons, ache for what we cannot do, but there is a day when the sun finally shines. We can make it. Time heals more quickly when we decide to let it. It is written that any man can make a mistake, but none but a fool will continue in it. This is a new day; live it fully.

The Great Spirit Chief who rules above all will smile upon this land . . . and this time the Indian race is waiting and praying.

CHIEF JOSEPH

March 23

The winner carries with him the quiet knowledge that though he has heard every argument, faced every opponent, felt every criticism, there is no turning back and no accepting defeat. An outraged Crow warrior spoke to those who were withholding food and goods that belonged to his people, "I am not a chief, but I am a warrior. I see that my chiefs all hang their heads down awaiting some reply from their father (the commanding officer), as they do not know what to do nor say. But I know what to do! Hold up your head when you speak to chiefs and warriors, look them in the eye! Goods were promised here and they will go no further!" And the goods went no further. Even a loss would simply be a delay to this Crow. It is a matter of how deeply we believe in what we are doing. Telling a winner that something won't work— just won't work!

Hold up your head when you speak to chiefs and warriors!

CROW WARRIOR

March 24

Evening walks have a beauty all their own as the sun moves through one phase after another, coloring and shading the fields and woods. Although the air is still wintry at times, the calendar says it is spring—good enough to stir up anticipation. The sunset changes from pale pink touched with gold to lilacs and purples and deep blues. The hills along the horizon have the deepest colors, all shades of Indian *gi ga ge* to match the red earth, the red skin. Above the darkening shadows, clouds like long tresses of silky hair spread out to the evening star. Everything gives way to that last bit of color, the burning embers that fire the distant hills—and then the velvet hour. Silence reigns. A coyote's long, thin wail tells the world that night has fallen.

I know every stream and every wood . . . like my fathers before me, I live happily.
    TEN BEARS

March 25

A herd of Jersey cows feeding in the meadow is reason to think wealth. Their milk is rich and they give lots of it. But there alongside of them is a patch of coreopsis—golden flowers by the thousands. They come again every year and bloom profusely even when a stretch of dry weather persists. Wealth includes many different things to fill many different needs. The Cherokees call it *nu we hna v i,* and to them the most important wealth is that which feeds the spirit— whether it is a field of coreopsis, a bank of oxeye daisies or a clean, flowing creek for good fishing. The cows, the milk, the provision for what we need to live are all important, but the Creator was generous in the necessary things—and then he gave us lots of little extras. The extras may be flowers or moonlight when the whippoorwill calls, or music. But it fills a need almost too deep to explain.

I want to roam the prairies. There I am free and happy.
    SANTANA

March 26

To be convinced that we are not alone in whatever place or situation we find ourselves is to have wisdom—exceptional wisdom. But when that wisdom is there and nothing can shake it, a need to share is strong. Everybody doesn't have the gift because everyone doesn't want it. Some can't even believe that anyone else has it. So, we should never try to convince them. If we are convinced, then, that is sufficient evidence, and other things will add to it as we go along. The Great Spirit speaks to us in sweet languages, so unique we cannot miss the import of what is said. To receive such a gift can change a situation from deep fear to one of total contentment and love.

I heard the mockingbird singing in the moonlight. I knew that moment that I would get well.

LONE WOLF

March 27

When we were born, we could not walk or talk or even focus our eyes. But the ability to do all these things and more was born in us. By continual effort, we still grow and learn and develop our identities. We learned early that we were not a bird and not an animal. And this is where personality begins to question—then, what am I? Who am I? Why am I here? Is this an identity crisis? No, it is a belief crisis. Every person has a hard time believing he has a specific reason for being here. Some have such a hard time believing that they go out and demand what others have. They see themselves outside the circle—not believing their own words and beliefs put them where they are. To a Cherokee status is freedom to move, freedom to achieve honor within himself, freedom to worship, and freedom to do what is right without ridicule.

They (the Cherokees) are apt in catching the spirit of growth. . .

March 28

Few sounds in nature are harsh. Even the rolling thunder that rumbles across the sky has solemn beauty. The wind makes whistles in the treetops and wild birds warble like rivulets of water that make harps among the shallows. The frenzied crash and blare come from man. The woods comfort with their sounds. A tiny yellow warbler with black wings sits in the redbud tree and makes the sound of an astral flute, a clear call for peace and harmony. If the bird wants a tranquil place—how much more we need it. A wet-weather spring feeds the ground from beneath, giving ferns moisture and life. In the rainy season the water flows and the delicate fronds mingle with the water creating a swishing sound. Surely we can absorb the serenity to heal and soothe our souls.

Creator of the world, Maker of all men; Lord of lords, my eyes fail me. . . for the sole desire to know thee.
INCA HYMN

March 29

Nothing ever remains quite the same—but a time comes when we have to follow new guidelines and think new thoughts and do new things. It does not take a superhuman, but it does take a believer—a worker with ears to hear and eyes to see—not just the physical but the spiritual. We cannot take for granted that any other human can have accurate perception and spell things out for us. The miracles are not all in other heads, other hands, other methods. There must be a burst of inner fire that sparks a miracle, that opens a door to a greater life, a greater calm. We are never so blind as when we close ourselves off by our critical views, our hardened hearts, our failure to perceive the greatness of gentle things. O friend, look away from lack and need and pain. Alter your vision and it will alter life.

O, great blue sky; see me roaming here. I trust in you, protect me!

PAWNEE

March 30

Innocent people tend to fall in line behind a person with the magical quality of arousing devotion—even when they do not see the ultimate destination. They simply follow. Their glee in being in a parade makes it seem to bystanders that they are left out if they do not follow too. As painful as it is to admit it, this is the vanguard of massive ignorance. Know what the parade is all about. How sad if we thought we were in the line to get freedom and discovered we were in the slavery line. We have to think for ourselves, as words deceive us unless we know what they mean. Our enemy is not always flesh and blood, but *a da lo nu he di,* which means deceit in Cherokee, and trouble in any language. Make it a point of knowing what and who can be trusted. There are many sources but only one Great Spirit.

Too many have strayed from the path shown to us by the Great Spirit.

SEQUICHIE GRANDFATHER

March 31

Be strong, be of good courage—so much we worry about will never happen. Put things in order, change what needs to be changed, but begin at once to count the *wi tsa to li gi*, the blessings that the Cherokee knows must be told again so we will not forget. Forget the past by which so much of life is marked. Painful things happen—and we take a little of all of it with us. This is a new day, *i ga*, a new time to be renewed. The more we let yesterday's unhappiness slide away, the sooner we come into the fullness of the present. Sorrow will fade. The new hour will bring new experiences, new jobs to do, and even a few negatives may line up to be counted. Don't do it. We can begin at once to call for what we want. We will coax all the sweetness out of every hour and it will sing for us like a bird.

We can't go back. The bridge is gone.
STRONG EYES

A P R I L

Tsi law'nee
Flower Month

*It seems to me that the rulers of the
Cherokees have sufficient intelligence
to see the utter imbecility of placing
any further reliance upon the
Supreme Court...*

GOVERNOR WILSON LUMPKIN
GEORGIA, 1831

April 1

In ages past, our old ones were the story-tellers. This was the way things were passed along to the generations that followed. For this reason the aged people made it a point to remember every detail so they could relate it at a later time. They were the word and picture carriers making history and spiritual values alive and important. In recent times we have made our old ones think they are not so important. We spoof their stories and make them feel foolish. The truth is that we are ignorant of what is precious and how to *a da li he li tse di*—appreciate age. Rigidity can creep in and set even the young mind if there are no soft memories, no laughter, no times too deep for tears. Age is grace—a time too valuable to waste.

We can get over being poor, but it takes longer to get over being ignorant.
JANE SEQUICHIE HIFLER

April 2

Wat we know in our heads is not always workable until we get it down in our hearts. The heart is the very core of us—the spirit, the vital *u li s go li yv*. Some call it the subconscious, the file room of our experiences and beliefs—the substance of who we are. Sometimes we file things in this inner-storage that are not to our benefit—fear for the most part. And fear is the subtle destroyer of the human spirit. But there are other things there as well, some of it information we neither remember nor even know we have recorded. Like old files, it needs to be cleaned out. But how can we clean out what we do not know we have? By self-monitoring, by plumbing the depths in writing, drawing out our own thought the way we prime an old pump to draw up water. It takes honesty spiked with a good sense of humor. Getting to know oneself is worth the effort.

Again . . . I recall the great vision you sent me. It may be that some little root of the sacred tree still lives.
BLACK ELK 1912

April 3

Why must we judge ourselves by what someone else is saying? They only think. Is it possible to fit our lives into the narrow confines of theirs? Let us search our souls. We have spiritual connections uniquely our own—deeper in many ways than those of people who want us to be like they are. But there is no way we can be like another person. We can only be better people in our own way. We know right from wrong, regardless of how the world-at-large has tried to condition us. Nothing can keep us from hearing our own voices of common sense—nothing, that is, but the noise and clamor of outside voice. And yes, maybe some are inside. But they have no good purpose; they mean to destroy. We need not dally with trouble. We can refuse to be a part of anything that was not a gift of *Galun lati*—the Great Spirit.

To fight is to forget ourselves as Indians in the world.
    MONTEZUMA

April 4

Our choices have brought us to this place. Other people affected us to some degree, but never so much as what we chose to do and how we choose to react. We are at the point the Cherokees call the hour of *tsu du go ta nv*, the place where we decide who is to sit at the forefront of our lives to guide the way. The hardest part is to stop thinking dilemma and start thinking and talking solutions. There is no room in problem solving for self-pity, not even revenge. Past events may have been wrong, but now we have to see it as change, not always our doing, but we have to handle it anyway. It is here that we decide to be happy, to be examples so that younger ones will want to follow. It is a worthy thing to be a good example. We may never know who will be watching.

Convince the world by your character that Indians are not as they have been shown.
JOHN ROSS

April 5

Power of some kind affects everything we do. But this power is not political or electronic so that one little glitch can wipe it out in seconds. The real power is what the Cherokee calls *adadolisdi*—which is prayer. Quicker than lightning, if it is handled the right way it can do anything. Born of spirit, this power is dynamite. It does not rely on outside currents of energy to keep it going, but thrives on self-generated faith that is properly fed and well-kept. We have no idea how dynamic this inner power is until we begin to rely totally on things and people outside ourselves. It is then that we feel the lack of joy needed to connect us to powerful *adadolisdi,* the language of love and worship. We can overcome the impossible with fire and mettle. We can grow in stamina with every breath—when we learn to use the power that is within us.

We may quarrel with men about things on earth, but we never quarrel about the Great Spirit

CHIEF JOSEPH

April 6

There are times when it pays to take a second look—to really pay attention to those things that cross our paths. We may have already missed a wonderful experience by hasty judgment. When quick judgments are made from a limited point of view, the good qualities of anything are hidden. It is essential to look beyond first impressions if we are ever to find a rare jewel. Even *Galun lati* is helpless to send us blessings if we are dull of spirit and incapacitated by our own smart minds. In our "expert" attitudes, we sometimes allow the very things that would make us peaceful and happy pass by without lifting a hand. Wisdom is being able to see quality in the rough—and then being gentle and patient enough to shape it to perfection.

How can we trust you? When Jesus Christ came on earth, you killed him and nailed him to a cross.
    TECUMSEH 1810

114

April 7

It seems only yesterday when the first cold wind blew in and laid flat the wild rose and turned the canes gray. Leaves turned and dropped. Snows fell and drifted. Winter threatened to last forever. But it didn't. Spring runs in and out like a child opening and slamming a door just to irritate us. The birds are flirting and meadows abound with baby calves in their first days. It is a time of change—not only in nature but in us. We enjoy that breaking point between late winter and early spring. In our mind's eye we know where the wild phox will spread its fragrance and the oxeye daisies will crowd the narrow path. It is with the same eye that we see ourselves blooming with health and prospering beyond our dreams. Only those who walk under a cloud miss the joy of this time, the open meadows and greening hills.

Oh, give me a home where the buffalo roam, where the deer and antelope play . . . Where seldom is heard a discouraging word and the skies are not cloudy all day.

ANONYMOUS

April 8

Peace of mind is better than gold and just as precious. But unlike gold, peace comes when we ask for it and let it happen—not when we go in search of it. We look for a time to be peaceful. But what may seem to be a waste of time can be just what we need— a spot of sunlight, soft breezes, the sound of locusts humming in the night. The little things calm us and bring us rest. But the best comes when we release our hold on little cares, the voices that tell us how bad things are in the world—and just let peace seep in. Nothing so becomes us as stillness and quiet serenity. Nothing so aptly furnishes the background music like sounds of nature, the mockingbird's midnight song that expands our boundaries and enchants our hearts.

We are a part of the earth, and the earth is part of us.
SEATTLE

April 9

A problem of recent times is that we do not have a set of values by which we can live. If we are to live well and be reasonably happy, we have to have an idea of who we are and where we are going. There must be rules to guide us. *Tsu gv wa lo di i* to the Cherokee means a definite standard by which to live, even when the values of others change by the hour. Without it, we are rafts on a high tide with no direction and no control. If the standard is missing we go with whatever comes along. Even if rules are self-made and are late in coming, if they come at all, it is worth the effort. And if we hold to them with a passion, they will be worth whatever we had to do, whatever we have to give up, to follow.

When a child, my mother taught me . . . to kneel and pray to Usen for strength, health, wisdom, and protection.

GERONIMO

April 10

There is a delightful piety involved when the other person is caught in wrongdoing. Sometimes we don't give much thought to the idea that someone made a mistake. He should have been more clever! Far too many get a lift when someone falls. It makes the sideliners look so good, and self-righteousness flows with great solemnity. But when the limelight hits home and attention focuses on a closer problem—where did all the compassion go? What is happening to human kindness? After all, are we not all too human not to err? Kindness is a two-way street. Harsh judgment and joy in seeing someone else hurt because they seem to deserve it, opens the door to let others judge us. So, then, where is all the compassion?

Little pot, do not call the kettle black until you have been in the fire as long as he has!

SEQUICHIE GRANDMOTHER

April 11

If the wind were a person, we would probably say something unpleasant about him. The more we try to ignore it, the more it seems to intrude, blowing away the cherry blossoms before we have seen them, whipping the lilacs and irises when their exquisite beauty is at its peak. But the wind is like circumstance; it serves a purpose to make the season go forward. It carries seeds of wildflowers and drops them in unexpected places to please us. It helps to unfurl the new leaves and to bring rain. Changes, like the wind, have to be endured at times. But eventually we understand and often like the results. It requires our patience—which gives us time to prepare for what is to come, the same way we have patience with what the Cherokee calls *ga no le s gi*, a windy person that blows and goes but means well.

As there is no alternative between a falsehood and a lie, they (the Cherokee) usually tell any person, you 'lie,' as a friendly negative to a reputed truth.

ADAIR

April 12

Something small so often comes to rescue us at a crucial point of making a mistake. How very much we wanted to react violently—to respond in the same manner in which we were approached. But somewhere deep inside, a gentler voice asked, "What is that to you?" Why be the other half of disagreement? Even an animal is smart enough not to run into a place where it can get tangled in a trap. Most arguments are traps of one kind or another. But relax right out of it. Let go, and realize that what is happening should be avoided like poison. The *atiyosdi*, the argument or disagreement, is on the other side—leave it there. The best revenge is to refuse to fight—and it brings to mind what someone said, "If you argue with a fool, you will end up being one."

I will fight no more forever.
CHIEF JOSEPH

April 13

The quiet companionship of a comforting person is like balm to the soul. Like Mother Earth, she absorbs the shock of pain and erases the wounds, and even the scars, with time. These kindred spirits seem to be able to take our hand and walk with us through the difficult places they have already traveled. They keep us from the loneliness that pervades our experiences, waiting for a word that we have passed through safely. And best of all, they never bring it up again but let the past take care of the past. Their eyes are on tomorrow, their hands on the present time so that we never hear empty echoes and are never reminded that we were unhappy. And then, we, in quiet ways, can reach back and take someone else's hand.

I take you by the hand with all my heart . . . you have spoken comfort to us.

LITTLE BEAVER'S WIFE.

April 14

Great strength exists in the smallest things. The spider's web is so exquisitely formed, a fragile, gossamer remnant. But it is stronger in proportion to size and weight than the finest steel. The hummingbird's wings send out impulses strong enough to resemble the throb of a tiny highspeed engine—but early on, it was thought that because of the way its wings were constructed it could never fly. Love can be a mere glance, *di ka nv to di,* a brief word, a silent touch. But it reaches past time and space and mere existence. Prayer, short, deep—a word from the depth of heart and spirit can work miracles and change a whole world.

There is something that whispers to me . . . to listen to offers of peace.
LITTLE TURTLE

April 15

Think and talk pleasant things. When pressures are too much, turn around and think and talk on another subject. Most of us are victims of our own emotions. We allow them to take over our peace of mind and there is nothing left to do but cry. And what we worry about becomes so real, so intense, that we believe it in all sincerity. The Cherokees say this is *v yo-ho wa yi gi,* something that is not true. When we are provoked to be negative there is no point in berating ourselves. Rather, say, "This is not acceptable. This is not my way and I refuse guilt, refuse being overwrought, and that is the end of the conflict."

You have spoken words of comfort . . . as though the Great Spirit was speaking through you.
    LITTLE BEAVER

April 16

April is the color of jonquils, the fragrance of hyacinths, and the dewiness of violets. The sunlit meadows are carpeted with tiny blue flowers, and along the ravines wild strawberries are as sweet and tart as April air. We forget that while the earth sleeps, life goes on, growing, developing, spreading, until at the right moment it reveals itself in glorious colors and shapes. A few short weeks ago everything was brown and somber. Now the colors are radiant and the very air is tinted the color of new leaves. A new aura outlines the distant hills and only human beings have to see and taste and stir themselves to new life.

I love the land. . . the trees which cover it, the grass growing on it.
    Como

April 17

Ｗe want to do the right thing, say the right thing, be the right person. We try to be in tune with life, to find harmony within to blend with all that surrounds us. It just seems that so much has been borrowed from us—time, concern, spirit—until we cry for restoration. Like children, we want to ask, "Are we happy yet?" Is there a time of rhythm and order and an even beat, so that we may walk without running, laugh without tears, care without fear of giving too much? Yes, beyond the slightest doubt we can renew and we can overcome the feeling of being totally taxed to despair. Speak to yourself, said the little Cherokee grandmother. Tell yourself you are *u wo du hi*, fine looking, and your surroundings will see it and want you to be happy. In other words, change your attitude and the world will respond.

Why do you take by force what you could obtain by love?

POWHATAN

April 18

The voice of doom is loud in our land. It is predicting unheard of fears and possibilities. But we have the antidote in our mouths—our words. Words are powerful, able to turn away the negative thoughts and words of those who have no purpose but to degrade. We don't have to let other people decide that we are victims of every attack, every disease, every wrongdoing. Our *u ni ne tsv* (words), say the Cherokees, are mighty to pull down anything or any person that lies in wait to harm us. Life and death are truly in the power of the tongue—and our part is to study the use of words and their effect on us. We know what it is to hear words of courage. It is light entering a dark place and we hear as well as speak.

Give ear, I am the mouth of my nation.
KIOSATON

April 19

A woodland path is good medicine for a weary walker. Soft, rolling steps along the path do not interrupt the harmony of the woods. Even the snort of the doe before she bounds away is to tell her fawn to lie low. Many pauses give time to hear and see in detail the call of a busy titmouse and the highpitched whistle of the finch. This is Cherokee paradise—to stand quietly in aged timber and be so much a part of it. Even the tiny creek plays water-harps as it winds its way around clumps of dried leaves and slips over round stones that are a part of its past handiwork. This is a green cathedral with shafts of sunlight cutting through thick foliage to turn droplets of water into prisms of color. Nothing is out of place—not even the walker.

Indian's pictures last forever.
INDIAN GUIDE, PIPESTONE CREEK, 1882

April 20

An idea is a rare butterfly that leads us through visual and spiritual experiences, and brings us out of the woods changed and ready to do something we never dreamed possible. Most people catch hold of ideas and immediately say they take too much time and money to be worth the effort. A quick excuse has cut more people out of doing a profitable and rewarding deed than all their other work put together. Fear of failure chips away at self-confidence until there is no heart to step into new territory. One needs the mind of a child to forget what happened an hour ago. If we cannot forget, we put it aside until we get to a place where we can understand. Otherwise, our creativity knows no bounds. We are caught up in a world of imagination—the thing that blesses all great inventors—playing what-if and finding great treasure.

The Cherokees' tribal vitality would again save them, as it had throughout their history.
STEELE-WOODWARD

April 21

Peace like a river . . . Feel it, think it, see it. Peace that flows not in wild frothy turbulence but in smooth currents that will not toss the smallest boat. Think of peace that so permeates our entire being, a peace that is closer than our hands and feet, closer even than our breathing. *To hi ge se s di* came with great difficulty to the Cherokee. Peace on earth seems distant to almost anyone in any age, but it is still sought, and the lack of it still affects each of us personally. Stress raises our blood pressure, makes our hearts race and our ears roar with panic. We can stop right here and now and put it all down. Speak the words of old that stopped a storm, "Peace be still." It worked centuries ago and its power is still intact. Say it many times a day to stop the negative flow that intends to sweep us away.

I am Dekanawidah, and with the Five Nations confederate lords I plant the Tree of the Great Peace.

IROQUOIS LEGEND

129

April 22

In the seventeen hundreds, the Natchez mother of a young chief suspected he had become involved in a conspiracy and was being used by his elders to do wrong. She said, "Open your ears and listen to me. I have always taught you not to lie." Liars are lost in a world of their own making. We have seen it glamorized in a world of make believe until the real world has difficulty telling the truth, even when there is no need to lie. Even the little white lies thought so harmless are barriers, wrongs, that stand in the way of honor. A lie, in whatever form, is deceit, and deceit is a major block to answered prayer, to friendship, to stable lives. The biggest lie of all is that lying is in any way harmless. Truth sees through the thin veil of a lie and all credibility is wiped out. But Truth stands forever.

I have always taught you that a liar is not worthy of being considered a man. . .
STUNG ARM

April 23

Some of the best successes have been those that came on the spur of the moment—something we caught hold of and lightly carried through with the air of having done it a thousand times. How does it happen, when we so often hear that all-too-familiar thud? It is the consensus of the Cherokee that the heart, the *u na wi*, the spirit of anything should not be heavy when we are dealing with the substance of the Great Spirit. The underlying *di ka no di*, or material to work with, must be handled and carried with hands that *a da la du di*, worship the Source of light and not the darkness. When we are too serious about our own importance we labor under heaviness, and the way is so slow we begin to doubt. Never doubt *Yoweh*, and the Great Spirit will carry through.

You said you would enlarge the fire. . . add more fuel to make it brighter. . .
CANASSATEGO 1742

April 24

The wild pink verbena that grew so profusely along the slopes have moved to another area. In their place are yellow flowers, unfamiliar but like sunshine after a shower. A familiar saying is that the more something changes the more it stays the same. Flowers, like people and circumstances, change so swiftly and unexpectedly that it seems like the very foundation of the familiar is moving and changing before us. The Cherokees call this *a ma yi*, creek water. It is always moving and changing before our eyes. Nature reminds us to renew our minds—to update and enlarge our vision instead of accepting the daily changes of the world that come to nothing. No one has ever been so perfect that he cannot surpass himself and bloom more brilliantly in another area.

When we lift our hands we signify our dependence on the Great Spirit.
BLACKFOOT

April 25

Someday, we will know how to take living in stride, to sidestep a great many things and completely ignore that many more. Sometime, we will learn to pay less attention to the imagined and stop fussing about things we had nothing to do with in the past—and cannot change significantly in the future. One day, like the elderly Cherokee, we can say, "So long a time since I see you...I don't care anymore." Soon, we will rid ourselves of things we saved for no good reason—and have room for what we really want. As soon as possible, we will worry less about trouble...knowing some people need it for their security. Very soon, we will sit together in the sun a whole day and just be happy that we can sit together in the sun all day and just be happy.

Even as you desire good treatment, so render it.
HANDSOME LAKE

April 26

Negative thinking is a habit that can be changed—if we really want to change it. It is too often like pressing on a sore spot just one more time to see if it still hurts. Most people's problems are found in areas of need—the need to have difficulty, the need to have something to deal with so they can feel needed and important. After all, what do we do when no one is depending on us? It is an innate Cherokee belief that we have no need to borrow trouble, *a to li s di*, no proclivity toward trouble. Let it stay where it is—or dissolve. If difficulty engages our eye, it may come to us. We can know happy things to fill our time. It is fatal not to want happiness and well-being enough that we invite it into daily living.

Though we are powerful and strong, and we know how to fight, we do not wish to fight.
THE CHEROKEES

April 27

Forgiveness seems to be continually with us—the need to forgive, to be forgiven, is directly tied to loving and being loved—or lovable. We sometimes love better at a distance. Time and space have a way of putting things into perspective so that we can see the right and the wrong to be able to forgive or ask forgiveness. We never gain ground as long as we are obstinate about forgiving. A grudge is a stone wall that forbids us to move in any direction. The Cherokees have labored long to understand the reason for the Trail of Tears—the same way other tribes have tried to understand. Life has a way of working itself out to certain ends, a time for everything, and what has been lost will be regained many times over. When? There is an exact moment. *Yoweh* knows.

When we are at peace we hunt freely, our wives and children do not stand in want . . . We sleep easy.

CHEROKEE

April 28

How frightening to be out of touch—but how normal! There are times and places we go through that are strange—both in feeling and understanding. We experience an uneasy feeling and want to rush back to the familiar—even though it isn't the place to be either. In growing, we go through strange places and think unusual thoughts. Fear of the unknown has made us wary, questioning, reaching for something to steady us, to give us direction and purpose. But we must expand our spirits, enlarge our thought to accept or reject what we have yet to learn. The American Indian has known the strangeness of new lands, new customs, has fought and lost—only to fight and win. Some are caught in between, but their staying power is in the Great Spirit who ever holds our hand and intercedes on our behalf.

I would that I could make the red people as great as the conceptions of my own mind, when I think of the Great Spirit that rules over us all.

TECUMSEH

April 29

Life stirs up our priorities—makes us think beyond our usual knowledge. There are enormously important things basic to all of us such as the family. The family as a whole is important, and so is each individual. Family makes us consider health and spirit and the capacity to take care of ourselves. The invisible circle gathers all we love close to us. But the final arc involves the making of who we are personally. Each person must know contentment, must be in awe, reverent toward the spiritual, recognize truth, and not go strictly by the depths and height of feelings. Searching for happiness leads us far afield when the search is for self, for a divine connection, a knowing that we are indeed divinely centered. We are a part of the earth, part heaven, one with every living thing. For this reason we love. The ga *lv quo di*, the precious, the dear truth is that we love.

It is the command of the Great Spirit, and all nations and people must obey.
BIG ELK

April 30

Those of us who have seen a grass fire know that when one flame is smothered, another can break out in a different place. It takes trained minds to perceive where the next will happen—not so different from our daily lives. Sometimes it is hard to do anything new because of the emergency work. This is all a part of the business of living. We never quite reach perfection—not all at once. Even if we do, we are off to something else that needs more help, more work. If it were not for the moving and stretching of time, perfection might become a dead nothing. The Cherokee would tell you not to build your campfire near loose tinder. What earthly purpose is there in starting a fire with a match or a tongue, in places and in ways where we have no business?

No one ever saw an Indian destroy something the Great Creator gave to man for his needs.
RED FOX

M A Y

Ana-sku'tee
Planting Month

*We, the old settlers here in council
with the late emigrants, they are
perfectly friendly towards us . . . we
have full confidence they will receive
you with all friendship.*
SEQUOYAH

May 1

A country road in May hums with activity. Bees comb the clover fields for nectar. Buttercups and dayflowers open to the sun and a mockingbird sets out to mimic every sound it has ever heard—even the baby chick. Wild onions and pink verbena share space and the buttery blooms of buffalo peas nod in spring breezes. Only now the air has warmed to the sun and the plants and leaves of oaks grow so much overnight that the sky closes in like a cocoon. Now is the time to slow down and enjoy the minute changes as they come hourly, the scents, the roadsides filled with new plants, and the green hills and valleys. They come quickly, the *di ga ne tli yv s di*, changes, that sometimes mature before we see the difference. If we are not careful, our clouded thought and vision shut it out until we have missed the best part.

This brings rest to my heart. I feel like a leaf after a storm, when the wind is still.

PETALASHARO

May 2

I s it true that if we get past this one hard place, all our problems will be solved? But each day has its share of such places—if not in our lives, then in the lives of those we care so much about. We are so interchangeably connected that whatever touches one of us touches us all. *A ne lv to di,* one strong effort, one day at a time, one step, one question, Are we reliable? Or do we get other people to cover our tracks so that we can go on doing what we want to do? When a hard spot, a habit, an addiction dogs our tracks, it is because we have not made up our minds to turn around and face it. Trying to make it acceptable only robs us of what we need most of all—to love ourselves and to respect ourselves. But we cannot do it alone. Only the Great Holy Spirit, and He alone, can give us the power.

The Great Spirit does right. He knows what is best for His children.
SENECA

May 3

Living catches up with us quickly when we let everything become drudgery. We stop learning. We quit looking with interest, and we stop being aware of our own needs and feelings. Everything becomes routine and nothing new is on the horizon. We blame far too much on age. Age has little to do with the blue fog we let settle over us and the things we usually care about. It is our lack of energy brought about by our lack of vision. It is a lack of interest that dulls memory. *A ga yv li,* the elderly, are held in high regard in all Indian tribes. They have to remember so they can tell the young—and they would tell us to watch our mouths so not to speak negatively. They would tell us to renew our vision. They say our potential is unlimited and we will know when something or someone lights our candle.

What is life? It is the flash of a firefly in the night . . . it is the little shadow which runs across the grass and loses itself in the Sunset.
CROWFOOT

May 4

Little things speak to our hurts. Sounds, fragrances, music that would mean nothing to others, reach into our souls to do a work that the obvious could not touch. Simple remedies can heal the deepest ills—a smile, a contented whistle of a passerby, the sound of birds twittering at dusk—these things warm us and give us hope. But we have to listen for voices, inner and outer, to give us rest—and turn away the negative talk, the negative circumstance. We don't always believe we have a choice—but we have more space there to work than we know. We can no longer scoff at the power to help ourselves. We have a bigger hand in it than imagined, and it is our decision to get down to business and be open to help and healing from unlikely sources.

Day and night cannot dwell together. Your religion was written on tables of stone, ours was written on our hearts.

SEATTLE

May 5

Remembering can be painful and sometimes without any real benefit. But much of the time it helps us move ahead like a spur that tells us not to tarry but to go on and do what we have to do. It is far too easy to carry around a *u s ga nv tsv*, a false guilt, a wrong idea, to override our good memories. We lose sight of the positive things we have done and the happiness we have shared by recalling a thousand impossible wishes we wanted to come true. But it does no good to dwarf the present time because the past was not what we hoped it would be. We cannot help but recall things and times and people dear to us—but to remember them with pleasure does them more honor than to focus on what we did or couldn't do in the past.

Our bare feet are conscious of the sympathetic touch of our ancestors as we walk over this earth.

SEATTLE

May 6

When we let down our guard, habit is waiting to reclaim its territory. It seems innocent and it is so familiar that we seldom suspect what teeth it has! Once we decide to change something, we can't expect to do it in one great sweep. What has taken us over by such tiny degrees must be edged out the same way. The fact that we are taking small steps does not minimize a very great commitment. Little by little, we reform our habits, making sure we leave no void for any other bad habit to fill. If we have *a ne lo ta nv*, made an effort or tried to change and failed, it is probably because we tried to do it alone or denied the need to change. The Cherokee believes he needs a *u na li go sv*, a help or a partnership, to give him support. It may be another *v da di lv quo ta nv*, a special or blessed person that is grounded in the *Galun lati*.

I am tired of talk that comes to nothing.

CHIEF JOSEPH

May 7

If we ignore everything beautiful and look down the road to some future time, chances are it will be the same. This is the time, the *e to a,* the now, the present, to see the dearness of other people, the chance to be grateful—to enjoy. Why wait? Perfect times are elusive. They create an atmosphere that life should be lived on some high emotional level instead of experiencing the most ordinary times with the most extraordinary love. Time goes by. The peaks were not what made life worthwhile—but the in-between times that gave us a chance to stand in the quiet of a wooded glen, even if it is just in our hearts, and know that love made it all worthwhile. Love will continue to make each a giant of peace in our souls.

I want to tell you if the Great Spirit had chosen anyone to be chief of this country, it is myself.
SITTING BULL

May 8

There is something very good about suppertime. Suppertime is more than just a time to eat—it is warm with happy memories. A few sunny hours to run barefoot after school, a time of homecoming and hearing what everyone else did during the day. Suppertime means watching Grandmother make *digalvnhi*, Cherokee grape dumplings, and hearing her sing as she worked. A day, a time, an hour never stands on its own, but is bolstered by all those hours that have gone before. Nothing is ever lost—not even the simplest things—for time enhances what has been dear to us. We tend to look back and think something no longer exists. But it does, in all the lovely hours that wait for us—like suppertime—like singing in the kitchen and warm bread baking. This is not just memory, it is sharing life.

We do not want riches, we want peace and love.
    RED CLOUD

May 9

Sentences half spoken and beyond total hearing are the source of difficulty. Only in the bright light of reason and understanding can these cloudy mishaps be corrected. Some are simply tuned to hear the negative—even when it was never intended to be. They hear with an ear that is already bent toward trouble and only too willing to pass it on. We might consider what we want to hear—because everyone has moments when words tumble out with little meaning. Whether it is a slip of the tongue or simply filling in a quiet spell, we are sometimes guilty of speaking when we should have been listening. The tongue is a little member and sometimes kindles quite a fire when it should spit on the matches.

We are becoming like them . . . all talkers and no workers.

BLACK HAWK

May 10

We are complex combinations of many things. Mind, body and spirit, yes, but with all the height and depth and feeling that make up the three. If one of these is not kept in shape and made to be harmonious with the others, we are out of balance. There is almost always more interest in one part rather than seeing the necessity of developing the whole person. What reading a book is to one person equals running a mile to another. It is natural to do what pleases us and makes us feel worthy. The Cherokee claims that if you *tso tle s di,* sit down all the time or are idle in mind and spirit, the whole *i ya dv ne li da s di,* complex system, suffers. Once upon a time, Indian dancing served the whole person, worshiping, exercising, and activating the mind. True fitness requires it all.

We work as hard as you do! Did you ever try skinning a buffalo?

OURAY, UTE CHIEF

May 11

Honeybees that relied on early flowers in the garden can now feast all across the meadows. Red clover, honey locust trees, and rose-colored Indian paintbrush abound in clusters to feed the bees and give peace to the eye. An evening chorus of field sparrows trills in the wheat field and a nesting killdeer demands privacy by doing her broken-wing act to sidetrack walkers. The whole meadow teems with activity until dusk—and then a silence pervades, only to be broken by the throaty voice of the tree toad. It is common knowledge among the Cherokee that every animal, except man, knows the main business of life is to enjoy it, and he, the Cherokee, sides with nature.

Seed time is here but your grounds have not been prepared for planting. Go back and plant the summer's crop.

KEOKUK 1832

May 12

Country people do not find it strange to hear the pond is turning over. They know it is not doing a flip but everything that has fallen in it suddenly comes to the top. It is nature's way of cleaning house. It isn't pretty, but it does work. The whole pond of human affairs needs to turn over at times. When everything seems to happen at once, friends disagree, and co-workers are suddenly mired in stuff from the bottom of the pond, it is time to clean house. It isn't always *u wo du hi,* beautiful or pretty, but it does work. The best part is that it doesn't last long. Everything rights itself with time—for a while. It helps to know that when something unclean falls in the water, eventually the pond will turn over to get rid of it. It just takes time.

We took an oath not to do any wrong to each other or to scheme against each other.

GERONIMO

May 13

Sometimes it takes another person standing on the outside of our emotional problem to do for us what we can't seem to do for ourselves. We need those who can see beyond appearances and will let us lean on them until we are in control again. It isn't the Cherokee's natural bent to discuss a problem openly with anyone. Silence is not only golden, it is safer and does nothing to make a problem grow as he believes talking will. But he knows the time, the place and the right person will avail themselves to him, and then he can talk. It isn't that we fear showing a weakness, but that we know the power of the word to make matters worse if we talk in a negative way about our needs. Even prayer should not be to reiterate our wants. *Yoweh* knows what we need. *He* waits for our adoration and thanksgiving that the needs are already provided for.

There is a dignity about the social intercourse of old Indians which reminds me of a stroll through a winter forest.

COCHISE

May 14

How many times she called me to her side to share something beautiful—the glowing embers in a sunset, the call of a whippoorwill, or one of those rare moments when Venus draws near the new moon. How many times she held my hand to comfort me through hope and fear, birth and death, happiness and unhappiness. How many times she taught me that no one is ever alone. We are always in the presence of Father-God who loves us—no matter what might appear to frighten us. How many times she said, "You can do it!" and how many times she refrained from saying, "You'll never make it." And how many blessings I wish upon her—my mother!

I will come with my family and pitch my lodge in your camp, that others may see. . . you are under my protection.

Eagle Wing

May 15

Our willingness to work at whatever we can opens doors to new opportunities. Willingness breathes life into us and gives us vision. Hope is good but determination is even better. It sets the tone to move, to do the thing set out for us. And we can do anything when we do not stop to consider what if we were to fail, or what if we are not appreciated. Cherokee women were never considered inferior to the men. They were honored and respected and educated themselves so they could teach their children. It meant hard work and determination to perfect what they could so they could pass it on. Sometimes, the main objective of our work is not just to prosper us but to do a worthwhile thing well. We keep labor on a high level, never taking the easy way out. There is honor in work—even in the most menial job. Success is short-lived when the work is done for appearances.

If our children should visit this place . . . they may see and recognize with pleasure the deposits of their fathers.

SHARITARISH

May 16

There is a chance that a decision we make will lead us into battle, an inward and an outward battle against our own will and against the negative flow of the world in general. A cherished goal challenges us that we cannot do it—we can't possibly do what smarter people have tried and failed to do. But chances are we have a source of wisdom that others may not have had, though everything points to their advantages over ours. Maybe we have a source that is more reliable, that no weapon formed against us can prosper. Chief John Ross taught the Cherokees to be persistent. Not a moment could be wasted in apathy, but we had to be there with muscles and mind toned and ready. The tribe's willingness to follow through with honor and integrity helped us to survive.

Our cause is with God and good men, and there we are willing to leave it.

CHEROKEES

May 17

It is useless to put a warped container inside a good one in hopes of straightening it. It only spoils the good one. The stuff they are made of has to be workable if either is to be saved. We can be affected, even encouraged by outside influences, but real change is from the inside. It is possible to wait a long time for a situation to change so that we can change. It won't happen. We have to change first—our thoughts, our attitudes, and very often, our reasons. If we are ever to be totally free of *u tso a se di,* the Cherokee expression for miserable or unhappy circumstances, we will have to remold our own human spirit to the will of the Great Spirit. It is the only help that is not based on money or dependency on someone else who is equally weak.

Great Spirit, once more behold me on earth and learn to hear my feeble voice.
   BLACK ELK

May 18

Have we lost control of who we are? Have we allowed ourselves to get in a position of little or no control—believing that we must forfeit bits and pieces of who we are to get along? The one weapon against us that has the total respect of the world is the business of weight loss. Never have so many fought so long to lose so little. Think of the dollar value put on a pound of flesh—the hype, the remorseful tears, the acceptance that we cannot control our eating. Though over-indulging in anything is dis-ease, it is not disease. It is the silent enemy, the spirit of destruction that the Cherokee calls *u so nv i*, which is not good but downright evil. It is the enemy with no power except subliminal suggestion. But enter the Great Holy Spirit, and its great roar is but a pipsqueak. We have to care, but we also need to know the truth to be free.

When the Great Father sent out men to our people, I was poor and thin; now I am large and stout and fat. It is because so many liars have been sent . . . and I have been stuffed full of their lies.
    RED DOG 1870

May 19

Ⅰf there is one thing that scares us, it is the thought that any part of life has been wasted. We look back and ask why we let it happen—what was so important that it could steal our youth, our strength, our capacity to be somebody—to just be happy. Is it too late to begin again? Never. It may be with a different set of rules, a standard of values that has changed drastically, but begin again? Yes. Many have started over and have had more happiness and contentment in a short time than in all of what is known as the wasted years. Anyone who has ever traveled a trail of tears wishes they had known then what they know now. But we did not know, and life is not lived by hindsight. We did what we knew to do—sometimes with great ignorance. But if we know the difference now and want to begin again—then why not? And why not now?

Years of trial and anxiety, of danger and struggle, have maintained the . . . Cherokee people as a distinct community . . . and such must continue.

CHIEF JOHN ROSS

May 20

Many of us would gladly take the responsibility of hurt for those we love. We feel we would be more capable of bearing it, more apt to handle it. We want to leave them as unscathed and near perfect as possible. But we cannot take some people's problems. They must use their own strength and learn what is true and false in living. Not so different from us, they might not take the wisest steps. It may also be hard for them to believe that our experiences have ever been as wretched as their own. It is difficult not to cry with those we love. Our hearts cry, even when frustration makes our faces stern and stoic. But we have to allow other people to put down their feet and take a stand. How can they become strong in their own right if we try to be in their legs?

Sometimes we prayed in silence; sometimes each one prayed aloud; sometimes an aged person prayed for all of us . . . and to Usen.

GERONIMO

May 21

Many are gamblers without knowing it. They demand their right to do something—even when it is not expedient. We can insist on our right to turn at the stoplight, but if someone else has never heard of our right and takes his chances at going through, it is dangerous business. Having rights holds only if the responsibility of them goes with it. Sometimes a right is a privilege we don't dare demand. The Cherokee calls this *u na du da lv*, acting in a way that is mature and careful of others. Some people tend to believe they are above the basic rules of living. But when life drops a rock on the one who so freely takes advantage, it can be a well-deserved rock. It reminds us to stay within the limits of everything from good taste to common sense.

The good road and the road of difficulties you have made me cross; and where they cross the place is holy.
    BLACK ELK

May 22

The past is to be respected for its rich store of experience—mistakes and all—believes the Cherokee. In it are all the trials and wisdom of our elders, the timeless suffering and seasoning that came to us with a brave front. But we, with less experience and far less wisdom, question why they did certain things. We have only to look at our own recent history to know that many circumstances come in to dictate some of what happened. We do not relate it to our offspring word for word—why we did something, wise or unwise. It is better they take what we have learned and build on it. The young have a tendency to see themselves far more shrewd and able than their elders. But one day, they too will see and understand the patterns that have been laid down. They will forgive and hope to be forgiven for not being miracle workers. The fact that we are here with a load of experience and wisdom behind us speaks positively of the past.

Grandfather, Great Spirit, you have given me the cup of living water, the sacred bow, the power to make life and to destroy it.
    BLACK ELK

May 23

Pride so often makes it hard for us to ask forgiveness. Instead of saying we are sorry for a mistake, it is easier on the pride to pretend it did not happen and quickly change our behavior. Words are important in love and forgiveness—and courage. It is good to hear them—better to speak them. Forgiveness is not just to make someone else feel better about us but to help us think better of ourselves. To make amends, set things straight, is *go tlv hi so di,* to change—not just outwardly for effect but inwardly for good reason. When we forgive someone we stop resenting them. It takes a little while longer to forget—and even longer to forgive ourselves for having been so foolish.

We want to keep peace. Will you help us?
  Chief Red Cloud 1870

May 24

A thick layer of doubt like fog across the hilltops, can shut out the light. Without light, we are depleted of energy and vitality—and eventually hope. An elderly Cherokee woman said, "It is true that the Cherokee suffered when their houses and gardens and very way of life were taken from them. We loved the land and trees and treated them as family. It was not the Great Holy Spirit that caused it. It was the *a s ga na* (wickedness) of the world." It seems that no good time exists when we can despair. The Cherokees still dance—not pagan dances as the world once supposed—but to the Great Spirit in gratitude, the way David danced before the Lord. And it is high time we shout and clap our hands right in the face of trouble.

You have said to me. . .that I could send out a voice four times. . .and you could hear me. Today I send a voice for a people in despair.
    BLACK ELK

May 25

Greatness is in having a purpose—not in just having a personality. Purpose shapes personality, not the other way around. Chief Joseph, Chief John Ross, and Sitting Bull were all great leaders, but their central purpose was even greater. Every seed of knowledge, every ounce of wisdom, was to lead and guide their people. They were constantly reminded of how much was yet to be learned. When a purpose and a goal stand for the good of the people, it carries a seed of greatness. In its simplicity it has no time for constant limelight, but only to accomplish more and reach farther. In areas of service, doing something to help other people humbles willing workers. They know they only scratch the surface of what there is to do— and unbelievable barriers are set in their way by ignorant people.

We are peaceful, we are not aggressive. In this lies our strength.

AN INDIAN ELDER

May 26

Does a child look at an older person and say, "I want to be just like you"? Not usually. More than likely they say to themselves that they hope they are doing better than what they see when they reach the same age. It is a fear thought. Time is getting away and this is what I fear I will be. We are one with other people, we need each other, but we are not all destined to be exactly alike. Common sense and individuality were put in us when we were created—not to be idle but to be used. Why give in to every negative suggestion when all we have to do is tell ourselves it is not, and never will be, acceptable. Tradition is strong in the Cherokee family. Old ones are thought wise and they are respected. But we are all individuals with different gifts that are enhanced by heritage.

We never made any trade. Part of the Indians gave up their lands; I never did. The earth is a part of my body, and I never gave up the earth.

TOOHULHULSOTE

May 27

Suddenly the hour is gone—and it is anybody's guess what we did with it. Did we enjoy anything? *U li lo hv s gi,* pleasant times are for a purpose, the Cherokee believes. It is not just *u wo tiv di,* something to amuse us, but pleasure slows the heart, lowers the blood pressure, and gives ease to the mind. Something beyond the awareness tries to slow the human spirit from living so intensely. It is not natural to push the mind and body until such weariness takes over that there is no natural relief. A pause, a *a tsa we so lv s di,* which means a reprieve or rest, will give us strength and renewed vision. Without it, we are burned out and we enjoy nothing.

Lots of us may not have learned yet . . . we all have brains and are anxious to work.
    ASA DAKLUGIE

May 28

Too much is learned that adds nothing to life. With the advent of "tell it like it is" the flow of troubled water washed in a mountain of debris. The unlearned feel it necessary to empty their garbage into the ears of other people without considering whether anyone wants to hear it. *U yo tsv hi,* the Cherokee calls it—not music, not poetry, not gracious words—but pure trash. The container may be new and shiny and touched with bits of colorful paint—but inside is the same old decaying *ga da ha,* (spoken with disgust), and the word is filth. Little things reveal much about a person—but none more than what he talks about, what he laughs at, what he finds amusing—or even helpful. No matter how beautiful or handsome—the tongue tells all.

Yesterday I heard something that made me almost cry.
LITTLE WOUND

May 29

L ittle is more symbolic to the Cherokee than a crystal-clear flowing stream. The banks of such a stream have known the most meaningful prayers, the worship and gratitude of the innermost soul. It is here that the Great Spirit speaks to us in supernatural ways, *a da to li s to di* for the Cherokee. The stream not only cleanses and washes away wrong and error but it is the tongue over which slip the words that have been fed there by the last rain. The words are a direct form of communication to the Great Holy Spirit, Who so centers our lives. All rivers run to the sea—whether it is a person's life or the flowing stream. Some of it is turbulent, some peaceful—with depths and shallow places, with swift mainstreams and circling eddies. But it is always moving, always gathering into its flow the experiences that make us who we are.

The springs. . .to bathe in them gives new life; to drink them cures every bodily ill.
CHEROKEE WISDOM

May 30

When we have lived a long time with trouble we learn to recognize it a long way off. Sometimes it hides behind the look of serenity, sometimes in laughter—but nearly always in the way a person jokes. It takes some understanding, some *go li s di yi,* some recognition or reckoning, to sense the pain that is so well hidden. In such cases, it often takes one to know one. We need each other. This unusual ability to see and form a kinship with another person makes us friends and loving partners. We have to be true to ourselves, to keep a part of the innermost heart sacred. A friend knows and respects in us what he, himself, must have as well.

I speak straight and do not wish to deceive or be deceived.
COCHISE

May 31

In this age of defending and demanding rights, we are often faced with the question of who holds us back more than anyone else...and in all honesty we must admit we are the ones. We narrow our vision and develop helpless and hopeless attitudes to defeat us. And yet, we are the ones who speed us on as well. Our good attitudes keep us moving and active and able to do everything without reacting to the smallest incident as a barrier in our way. We are willing to work, to initiate and set in motion the good of life, and do it by not stepping on others. We keep a constant vigil over our thoughts and action. In this way we follow our *lo qui si*, star, and reach up that we may lift others up with us.

Misfortunes do not flourish particularly in our path. They grow everywhere.

BIG ELK

J U N E

Da tsalu'nee
Green Corn Month

*I am . . . the Cherokees are . . .your
friends. . . . Our wish is for peace.
Peace at home and Peace among
you . . .*

CHIEF JOHN ROSS

June 1

The morning is quiet and the high-pitched cry of the hawk carries clear to the quail and rabbits that rely on their sharp hearing to skitter out of sight. The hawk is hunting, and the small things of nature want no part of it. Threatening sounds—whether from a *t wo di*, hawk, or sirens, or angry voices—are frightening. As a child, a lesson in survival was learned when a rabbit ran the length of a field beneath a barbed-wire fence with a hawk in pursuit. The hawk was not about to fly into the barbs and gave up to hunt easier prey. The rabbit lay spent from fear, panting and gasping—but unafraid of a child that was no *adananuladi*, no threat or danger. It is easy to go weak from fear. But how many know where to run to when angry sounds threaten? The hawk does not hover over us but *Yoweh* does.

I hear nothing but pleasant words.
  Mongazid 1825

June 2

Late June evenings offer a variety of concerts to the lingering spirit of *Tsalagi*, the Cherokee. The songs of katydids and crickets rise to a crescendo and shrink back the way a tide swells and recedes. A sudden volley of hoots shoot through the woods and impatient shouts answer. The prairies lie quiet and serene beneath faintly showing stars until coyotes, most likely only two or three, howl like a dozen. The first high-pitched shout is like the head singer at a stomp dance, and then others join in before they stop as suddenly as they start. In the lull, the plaintive voice of the whippoorwill adds a sweet note. It has all been a *ga nah si daw*, a messenger or ambassador of good will—of peace on earth—not only to the *Tsalagi* but from the *Tsalagi* to all the world.

June is Da tsalunee, the Green Corn Month.

THE CHEROKEE TSALAGI

June 3

Big changes require many small ones. Any change seems sudden, regardless of how much we prepare for it. We wait for it, ask for it, expect it, and resent its intrusion. Change is needed to stay young and vital and moving. Without it we stagnate, lose our keenness of thought, and too often fall into melancholy. Even in the best of times change takes a certain amount of adjustment. Our biggest problem with change is that we expect it to be bad rather than something that will make us happier. To a *tsa su ga,* a flea, a dog is the whole world, says a Cherokee. As much as we like where we are, it isn't the whole world. There are bigger things—and better. We have to be able to see beyond the dog.

I have made myself what I am.
   TECUMSEH 1810

June 4

What is so strange about using our words to build? Doesn't it make more sense to build something than to tear down? Who is closer to us than ourselves—other than Above-the-Sky, *Galun-lati?* We spend most of our time listening to our own words—words that go into our ears to build or tear us down. Sometimes they whisper in our silent talk, sometimes we say them and they affect us deep in our hearts. Confidence may come because of what someone else told us, but it is maintained by what we tell ourselves. We boost it every time we say we can do what we once thought impossible. We lose it by confirming what fear told us is true. Talking can change our circumstances when we change the words.

Tecumseh said to Big Warrior, "I will stamp my foot on the ground and shake down all your lodges." (An earthquake struck and tumbled the village.)

June 5

Nothing equals the loveliness of a summer morning when the first rays of sunlight sweep a field of wheat ready for harvest. The honey-colored heads bow with the weight of grain and the moisture of dew. Few of us could miss the peace that comes when the first light breaks through the foliage at the far side of the woods. It beams misty shafts of gold into areas untouched at any other time of day. It passes quickly and leaves the need to see it again. A miracle happens with the morning light. Worried thought lightens with the trill of the summer tanager. The wild purple cone flowers make their appearance in the meadow—and so the day begins.

Warm as go gi a ga li s gv, the peaceful day begins.

Warm as summer sunshine, the peaceful day a leni s gv.

June 6

The mind is like a bag with a drawstring. When the string is pulled so tight that nothing can go into the bag or come out—that is nervous tension. The problem is held in and the solution is kept out. At these times it helps to walk—at least far enough to detach from everything that reminds a worrier that he is hemmed in. While the feet are busy, the mind relaxes—maybe not to the point of being tranquil but at least to be able to *adanv tesgv*, think clearly or work things out mentally. And during the walk, deliberately turn thoughts to vision—seeing every detail, every sunflower. Look at the shape of a leaf, the spider's web, and look for color, and be grateful for the ears to hear and the eyes to see. Nothing heals the spirit and opens the way like turning loose of a problem.

Neither anger nor fear shall find lodging in your mind.

DEKANAWIDAH

June 7

Confession may be good for the soul, but it seldom makes the one that heard it feel good. The need to clear the air or get something out in the open can cause a bigger rift than the reason for confessing in the first place. Words cannot be retrieved once they are spoken. They are gone and calling them back is impossible. Some weigh on people's hearts like *hi lv s gi nv ya,* many stones or heavy rock. Some are flung, like *di ga ti s di,* a spear, to wound. And most should never have been spoken. Life and death are in the use of words. If we feel the need to confess something, we should do it where the listener knows how to handle what we say. It is an unthinking person that needs to be relieved of a burden to the point of putting it on someone who may find it hard to bear.

He knew his words were bad; he trembled like the oak whose roots have been wasted by many rains.

KEOKUK

June 8

It is unfortunate when someone fails us, but it isn't as bad as when we fail ourselves. The minute we make a mistake or fall short, we begin to condemn ourselves. How could we have been so dumb, so inept, so careless? We are victims by our own mouths. It is too easy to make a habit of thinking we are second-rate, not quite equal to others. If we say it enough times, we think it, and it all feeds down into our hearts to surface again when we don't need it. Who can love us if we do not love ourselves? Who will build us up if we are busy tearing us down? Confidence is winning over self—not others. But we have to stir up the gift that is within us, see that we appreciate all the small things we can do well. We can only be what we give ourselves power to be.

These words are mine and they are true.
CHIEF MENINOCK

June 9

Near is the lion on our path. But if we turn around and face it straight-on, it will slink away. The sooner we learn that fear has no power but what we give it, the sooner we gain control of all our emotions. The *Tsalagi* may know fear, but his stoic expression will never reveal it. To a Cherokee, *u na ye hi s di,* fear or alarm, is the face of the enemy that tries to numb his mind and spirit to make it easier to conquer him. The lion's roar is silenced the minute we face it down with our own *ga na nv di s gi,* war whoop, that shows we mean business. We have no intention to stand still and let fear open the door to worse things. By the faith words of our mouths we turn away, not only the lion, but all it represents.

I turn with a shout that we are saved!
    STANDING BEAR

June 10

Ideas are like eggs in an incubator. They must be kept warm and protected until they have grown enough to hatch. Our need to *go wo ni ha,* talk on and on, can do away with a promising situation before it has ever had time to take form. Left to develop, it may have been a great blessing to many— but tampering with it in our belief that we can do anything and say anything aborts it. There is a time to speak and a time to keep silent, but it takes wisdom to know the time. Most things can only stand one telling, and it had better be where it stands a chance to survive. Until that time, don't talk, don't count.

Grandfather, Great Spirit, once more behold me on earth and learn to hear my feeble voice.
    BLACK ELK

June 11

There is an undercurrent that feeds us false impressions like a gentle trap that tells us we are doing right—because it feels right. Feelings are so easily manipulated they can't be trusted as a measure in anything. We stay with bad habits because it feels right. The habit comforts our feelings and the familiar touch makes us believe we can't give it up. But it is the path that winds back through the same experiences—almost like being lost in a jungle. We think we are on the right road out, until we find our own footprints going around and around. Whether it is a habit or a person, or a situation we are trying to escape, we have to know our feelings are not to be trusted. They keep us knocking on a door that seems like home but is simply the same stopping-off, *na hna i,* familiar place. Beware of feelings that deceive.

It has been said that there is no deceit in touching the pen to sign a treaty, but I have always found it full of deceit.

STANDING ELK

June 12

Personal balance, says the Cherokee, is a matter of self-restraint, steadiness and consistency. We like to think we have some of each. We want to believe we know a good thing when we see it—and because we can see it we can possess it as well. Balance means living *du yu go dv*, squarely, or with truth. It means seeing that what we believe and what we talk about dictate what we get out of life. If we short-change, we get shortchanged. If we whip and beat and scheme to get the better of someone, time will equalize it. No one really gets away with anything. We love to win, but if deceit comes in, so do all the factors of balance. A smokescreen blows away with the slightest change in pressure. We get what we give—good or bad.

Do not wrong or hate your neighbor; for it is not he that you wrong; you wrong yourself.
SHAWNEE CHANT

June 13

Part of the world's problem with education is that common sense cannot be taught. It is not a result of education but exists in spite of it. If something is missing in the handling of ordinary problems, it is usually common sense. Many are blessed with extraordinary charisma, the gift of grace or special qualities the Cherokee calls *a da to li s di*. But to be used to any degree, charisma must be backed by practical wisdom—common sense. We can be ready for anything and equal to anything if we are infused with the inner inspiration to develop common sense. The genius may know he has a fine mind, but common sense is needed to manage it.

While the Indians received us as friends, and listened with kind attention to our propositions, we were painfully impressed with their lack of confidence in the pledge of the Government.
     1876 Presidential Commission report

June 14

This is the age of questioning. Nothing can be accepted at face-value the way it once was. A man's word has been broken so many times that we are convinced no one can be trusted. But such evidence is not always true. Emotions and unrestrained imagination make us assume that certain people are not trustworthy. If we are going on hearsay we are in no position to judge. When enough time has passed we will know what is true. Until then it is wise to withhold opinions and refuse to believe the worst of anyone— even if something has given us reason to be suspicious. The loss is too great to *a da du hi s to di*, to accuse or make a charge against people, without knowing if it is true.

You have come here to buy this country of ours, and it would be well if you came . . .with the price in your hand.

STANDING ELK

June 15

When we lean solely on the past, we remember vividly the things that never were. If something was *u wo du hi*, beautiful, the present time fades in comparison. If it was bad, it too often consumes our joy in every new day. It is a daily matter to pick up the good and put down the not so good. We hope to preserve the precious and lose what oppressed our happier natures. But it requires us to monitor what we are thinking about and how we tell it—and not pull up the flowers with all the weeds. If we had the capacity to be happy at one time, we still have it. It is just that we have it in a new time, under new circumstances and with a spirit freed from the past. The worst slave is the one who dwells on and relives the past in all its murkiness.

I will not dwell on, nor mourn over, our untimely decay, nor reproach our paleface brothers for hastening it . . .

SEATTLE

June 16

Success or *a s qua dv*, as the Cherokees use the term, is a sense of doing something and having the rewards. But anyone has to take care that a little success does not weaken effort or steal initiative. Persistence must be our constant companion for however long it takes and for whatever it requires of us, to keep stretching our limits, refining our spirits, renewing our minds. Things have never been important to the Cherokee as much as land and home and family. But success means different things to different people. Nearly all agree that dignity and respect are symbols of success—and spiritual foundations are not just buildings or groups but an inner power and strength of an individual.

Among themselves every warrior is an orator. . .an excellent way to whet the courage of their youth.
    WILLIAM FYFFE

June 17

How would we feel, what would we be doing or thinking if we were not in this situation? Strange as it sounds, these are questions that can guide us out of a place that is testing us severely. Just focusing outside a limited position helps us to see ourselves delivered and well. We must see it by using the same what-if that is so easy for us in negative ways. *E gi ya ni ha*, we are called, says the Cherokee, to use all our mental and spiritual resources to see ourselves free. It is never that we are sick and trying to get well—but that we are well and something is trying to make us sick. If we have a problem with a positive vision, then we can go back to being a child. Children have no trouble pretending. It is fun, it is joyful, and it raises the level of awareness to a healthy high so the body and mind can take over and restore and renew.

House made of dawn . . . restore my feet to me . . . Happily I recover . . . my interior becomes cool . . . As it used to be . . . I walk . . . In beauty it is finished.
  NAVAJO PRAYER

June 18

Talking too much is a little like painting a picture. It is frequently what we leave out that makes it the masterpiece. We don't have to tell everything we think—nor use every color on the palette. Subtlety makes someone else think, and that is more important. Our tendency is to think that no one understands unless we spell things out for them. It is hard to keep our mouths shut when we want to say something so much—usually with a *da li s ga na ne hi,* irony or a degree of sarcasm, according to the Cherokee. Silence can be as unkind as saying too much but in the long run it serves a better purpose in preserving friendships. There is a time to speak and a time to keep silence, but it is a person of rare sensitivity who knows when the time is.

Tell your children of the friendly acts of Indians to the white people who settled here. Tell them of our leaders and heroes and their deeds.

INDIAN COUNCIL

June 19

Some of us have kindred souls that understand what we feel, what we think, and what we need. These special people seldom bother with a lot of talk—but their quiet companionship is balm to the spirit and enough without words. Wherever we are on the pathway—the Cherokee calls it *ga lo hi s di*—one of these special persons has known loneliness, felt the solitary hours, heard the empty echoes, and is there to mark the way for us. We are assured of company, told that we will make it—that we are almost there now. Suddenly there is a corner to turn, a light to shine, hope and a hand to support us. Then, in quiet communication, we reach back and take someone else's hand.

They were kind to me, those old men, when I was working hard to learn from them these sacred songs.
PLAYFUL CALF

June 20

Everything is fresh and new on a June morning. Someone performed a miracle while we slept. The air was cleaned to crystal clarity, the rising sun glistens on every leaf and blade of grass. The hills are new green from spring rains and the horses that graze there are sleek and shiny. Such rewards, such *a sa s dv*, are for the early riser, the one who greets the day with thanksgiving and praise. Regardless of how many tag-alongs from yesterday threaten, they cannot break the spell of the beauty at hand. Another opportunity, another splendid day that is so oblivious to the schemes of man. To go with it, to rise with the morning mist, is to know the freedom and restoration in the soul of the American Indian.

To the Indian, words that are true sink deep into his heart where they remain; he never forgets them.

FOUR GUNS

June 21

Chances are we never recall just when we made the biggest decisions in our lives—unless we can remember some of our quietest moments. We think of change coming with fanfare, but that so seldom happens. Most of the time we silently recognize the great things in our lives long before we bring them out to be known by everyone. It is hard to say just when the change began. Some of it is even *ga lv quo di*, sacred to us, not easily shared—nor wise to share, because it is our own that comes from somewhere deep within us. There is an inner life that makes changes easier because it prepares us to accept what we cannot change—and more importantly, to change what we can.

The whole world is coming. A nation is coming, a nation is coming. The Eagle has brought the message to the tribe.

WOVOKA

June 22

Habit so dulls the edge of observation that it is easy to pass a tree and never see its beautiful seasons—or be around another person for a lifetime and never see the beauty of the soul. We travel great distances to see something beautiful, and go to great lengths to get a glimpse of a famous person—but our immediate surroundings fade so easily. Familiar faces, *a da to la gi*, voices, the easy touch of hands—are all taken for granted. With a firm foundation they can be relaxed and confident, but we still need to stay alert to their importance. Even good habits can dull our awareness to things necessary and dear to us.

I know every stream and every wood. . . I have hunted . . . and lived like my fathers before me, and, like them, I lived happily.
    TEN BEARS

June 23

Attitude is everything if the day is to go well. If we require others to have patience with us and give us *u we to li s di,* the Cherokee word for pity or sympathy, then our minds are going to be on whether or not we get it, instead of on living well. We forget that we project to others how we want to be treated. Arrogance invites resistance. Hang-dog attitudes invite other sour and sullen looks and behavior. Good-natured people are always welcome and give peace to our minds. Whatever we are about, it is to our advantage to know the world is reflecting back to us the mirror-image of pleasant manners—or the stern appearance of touch-me-not. It takes so little to relax and enjoy, so that others can do the same.

I am old, it is true; but not old enough to fail to see things as they are.

WHITE SHIELD

June 24

At times an idea hits us with the terrific force of a high-flying jet re-entering our atmosphere. It takes hold of us and shakes us with the same sound force and it is very often just as startling. A softpedaling thought comes to mind and we acknowledge it only briefly, but it comes back again and again, until we stop to think about it. It pays to listen. All good things do not come with mind-smashing sound effects. Some of the best of life comes on soft shoes and barely brushes us. If we are alert, we may savor it for a lifetime. If we are crusty and hard to deal with, a splendid idea may go right by us and light on someone more sensitive.

I have heard your words—they have entered one ear and shall not escape the other . . .

SHARITARISH

June 25

Just when we think nothing is working there is a glimmer of light. If we could believe in our hearts that what looks impossible can work out, we could bear more easily with hardships. Living is like the weather. It has its surprises, its storms, its dry spells. But if we can hold on, it all changes. The changes come the way we change our minds—unexpectedly and sometimes for no apparent reason. But the reason, the *uyelvdvi*, real purpose is there. Every word we speak, everything we believe, builds our consciousness and makes us who we are. If we expect nothing good, it will oblige us. We are as unlimited as we say we are, and it is in our power to make the difference.

Will we let ourselves be destroyed in our turn, without making an effort worthy of our race?
TECUMSEH

June 26

Someone said it is impossible to spit in the same water twice when it is a flowing stream. It is all water under the bridge—running on down to the sea, merging with other rivers flowing in the same direction. All rivers run to the sea. We cannot stop them any more than we can call back some incident to change it. It is water under the bridge, and has gone to join all the other experiences until their identities are forgotten. There is no use in chasing what is past. We can only love and care for what we have at hand. What is better than to enjoy the present time, the present company? To see this time equally important with the past is to regain some of what we thought we had lost.

Although ice and snow may lie deep upon my wigwam, I should find a warm fire within.

TECUMSEH

June 27

Gentleness has amazing strength. Where some would dominate, others are sweet and compassionate and this gives us hope. A gentle person is cool, clear water on a hot day—a refreshing change from hostile attitudes. How many times we have met someone we wanted to admire but couldn't. They would not trust us to see beyond their protective walls. Caring and friendship was sorely needed but bitterly ignored. To understand these things makes us gentle. It gives us the touch we need with every age. Young and old yearn to hear a voice that tells them they are so important, so loved, that nothing could make us turn from them. A gentle word is warm sunshine to every heart, a touch that is never forgotten.

Truly, it is a pleasant sky above our heads this day. There is not a cloud to darken it. I hear nothing but pleasant words.

MONGAZID

June 28

Music is the universal language—a link between people who have no other form of communication. It even helps us to understand ourselves when it brings out an emotion that was too deeply buried. Music was meant to be an integral part of our lives. A familiar tune can sweep us back to another time or another place that we thought was lost. It is the harmony that helps us blend the old with the new and dilutes a bitter memory. Few important events are without music. Bands have rallied us to patriotism, hymns have helped us to be reverent, and the sweet song of a small child can cause a tenderness to come on the hardest heart. The Cherokee calls it *di ka no gi dv,* the music of the spirit—in the turtledove, in the mockingbird, in the gurgling stream.

I take you by the hand with all my heart because you have spoken words of comfort to us.
    LITTLE BEAVER'S WIFE

June 29

Doing wrong to someone is like throwing a rubber ball against a wall—it comes back with equal force. There is no telling where it will return to, so we have to keep a constant vigil not to be caught off guard. It is easier to wish someone well. It doesn't mean we are weak or defenseless but that if we kick at the mud we get it on us. And there are some muddy situations we should never try to contend with or understand. Whatever happens to one of us has an effect on all of us. We can't afford the luxury of wishing anyone anything but the best of life. The Cherokee calls this the best of all—*wi ta tse tiv i*.

For years I have been on other people's ground and trouble has always come of it.

TOOKLANNI

June 30

I f we could change one thing about ourselves to see the greatest gain, it would be to stop being the victim. Too many believe they are destined to be victims of broken relationships, disease, poverty, and overbearing personalities—and they say it over and over again. How we see ourselves makes all the difference. If being brow-beaten is security, we will always be the underdog. Day after day we throw ourselves into the path of what we think we deserve. But we can change that pattern. We can stop repeating what we have heard all our lives, and begin talking to ourselves with good words. We have hidden gold within us and as soon as we learn it, we will get out of the lunacy of being the perpetual victim.

We must help one another and the Great Spirit will help us both.

PIED RICHE

J U L Y

Tsa lu wa'nee
Corn in Tassel

*My people have kept me in the
harness . . . I have never deceived
them . . . I have done the best I could.*
CHIEF JOHN ROSS 1866

July 1

In these times of instant everything our patience wears thin when we have to wait. Who has not pushed an elevator button a number of times to get there faster? Waiting may well be the hardest work we do. We are less than tolerant of those who keep us waiting. Is their time more important than ours? So we keep pushing, racing our engines and taking chances in order to save five seconds. We can wait wisely—seeing that, sometimes, delays save us from a problem we could have met. How long has it been since we have had such a good excuse to just sit quietly and watch others trying to beat the clock. Time was when our mothers sat all afternoon and embroidered, while their heads and feet rested. Could we not take thirty minutes?

We are hoodwinked, duped more and more every year; we are made to feel that we are free when we are not.
         WASSAJA

July 2

To someone who likes to walk, all of nature is a miracle. The sights and sounds and fragrances are ever different and soothing to the spirit. But evening has a special charm when the sunset changes from phase to phase, coloring and shading the fields with an artist's touch. The sky is tinted with the palest pink that has edges of gold—and then, in a subtle movement, purples and deep blues darken the hills along the horizon. The wind-tossed clouds catch the last rays of sunlight, rose-red and wavy like strands of silky hair. Above it all, the evening star emerges cool and blue to dominate little by little. Earth and sky and all between have special times when everything else gives way to beauty. If only we could be so generous with one another.

Today you saw a deer bounding through the forest, he was lovely in strength and beauty, fleeter than the winds.

METHOATASKE

July 3

We are always rich when we have courage. It is not the circumstance in which we find ourselves but how we handle it that makes the difference. If nothing ever challenged us we might not know our strength— we might never feel the power to overcome something that gives us courage to tackle another *o.ta li,* mountain. Giving up does not come on us suddenly, but we cultivate it on a daily basis. Everything, success or failure—or even mediocrity—settles on us as we get ready for it. When we think and talk failure, it happens. When we think we can do something, we can do it. It takes as much effort to lose as it does to win—sometimes more. But to think courage, to think strength, is the breath of life.

Why don't you talk and go straight and all will be well?

BLACK KETTLE

July 4

Let our objective be our country, our whole country, and nothing but our country. And, by the blessing of God, may that country itself become a vast and splendid monument, not of oppression and terror, but of wisdom and peace and of liberty, upon which the world may gaze with admiration forever." Daniel Webster spoke those words, and he knew that America would have fine troops, great leaders, and excellent equipment, a combination that stands for freedom. Even though freedoms have been stretched to the limits in some areas, we operate on the basic premise that this is America and it still stands as an example to countries everywhere of what it means to be free. President Eisenhower said that whatever America hopes to bring to pass in the world must first come to pass in the hearts of the American people. It has, and it will as long as we ask God to bless America.

Every part of this soil is sacred in the estimation of my people.

SEATTLE

July 5

Remembering can be painful and sometimes without any real benefit. It keeps us feeling guilty and regretting so much that the good memories are washed out. It is easy enough to forget the good that happened, without covering the good with bad memories. No doubt, everything has not been ideal— but haven't we given enough thought to the unhappy times? It doesn't do any good to ruin the present time recalling what went wrong in the past. But we can begin to change. Maybe only a little at first—but honest effort has always changed things for the better and given us self-respect as well. Time grows more and more precious and what we do with it at this moment makes or breaks today and all our tomorrows.

We are not afraid to work and we are not afraid to do right.

TOOKLANNI

July 6

Influence is like the wild phlox that blooms in the woods. Its fragrance drifts toward us, but from where? The distinctive scent tells us it is phlox—or is it wild grapes or plum? In the final analysis we know we smell flowers, but the kind and the location remains a mystery. So it is with advertising or rumor or neighborhood gossip. We know something is going on, because we are being conditioned to take suggestions, to be open to so much we don't need and do not want to hear. The same influence operates in other areas—age and illness, loneliness and fear. We not only get it over the airwaves that something miraculous has happened, to be contradicted only days later, but we hear people boldly claiming disease in a joking manner. Influence is subtle like the scent of phlox—or is it petunias?

The Great Spirit has given the white man great foresightedness; he sees everything at a distance and makes the most extraordinary things.
   CROW BELLY

July 7

A difficult challenge does little harm in comparison to the uncertainty of what to do about it. To take action, or let it ride; to stay or to go, to ask for help or wait for new developments. Indecision can wreck our whole thinking process and stall us out at a time that we most need a clear head. Our emotions rise and fall—from do nothing to do something. One minute we have a clearcut answer and the next we don't know what to do. The Cherokee calls this *a si ni*, backward thinking, going forward and backing up. It doesn't get us anywhere. There is nothing wrong with questioning, but wavering gets everything out of focus. No clear picture comes out of a shaky camera. Taking an action with a calm mind helps to clarify and give stability to the next steps.

You might as well expect rivers to run backward as that any man who was born a free man should be contented when penned up and denied liberty.

CHIEF JOSEPH

July 8

It is not enough to make something look good. The underlying principle must be good. How else could nature produce such majestic landscapes? They were not created for us to look at and approve. They were created because the laws of creativity were good. Now things are made to be temporary—to self-destruct. If it doesn't work very long—junk it. No wonder there are piles of debris. No wonder relationships struggle. The underlying principle is too often based on the idea that if it doesn't work, get rid of it. Few things are as enduring as the hills, few things as calm and serene as the lake on a quiet day. But if we have no firm foundation on which to build, what can we expect but upheaval and having to begin again.

The earth is full of minerals of all kinds . . . the ground is covered with forests of pine . . . if we give this up . . .it is the last thing that is valuable to us or the white people.
    WHITE GHOST

July 9

When people are secure, they can let someone else have the credit for doing something worthwhile and not complain. Sooner or later, the truth comes out anyway. Life always balances the credit. People have thought many times they were getting something for nothing—but listen, nothing stands for nothing. There is always compensation. Call it what it is. The only thing we don't pay for is love, real love, which the Cherokee calls *a da ge yu di*. What we give, we receive. Life is reciprocal, it requires us to do the best we can and to leave judgment and balancing to Him Who works out all things to their perfection.

Tell your people . . . that since we were promised we should never be removed, we have moved five times.
    A CHIEF 1876

July 10

Now trends and new ideas interest us, but how we love the familiar. We like to keep those things that are dear to us, old songs, familiar places, the good faces. Most of us don't want to recapture the old times. They have served their purpose and we have put too much into what counts for us now. But when something familiar comes to our ears, or a certain fragrance touches our memory, we are suddenly back there and reliving old times. It is tiresome to be forever striving toward the future. The road is unfamiliar—and every inch of it will have to be tested and tried. And then something we know by heart rises to the top and it buoys us up and we are ready to go again. Sometimes it takes the familiar to help us appreciate what we have today.

Grandfather, Great Spirit, the good road and the road of difficulties you have made me cross; and where they cross, the place is holy.

BLACK ELK

July 11

As unlikely as it seems at times, there is always a way—even a better way. If we can keep on working and using our vision, there will be solutions and they will not fail. Our limited view can make us believe answers must come through certain channels. It is hard to stop thinking that one particular way is all there is, that we have no choice. It makes us rely on a crust of bread when we could have a feast. If we want a breakthrough, we need to take off our blinders—stop pressing our minds into tiny molds that have no room to expand. Allow, even encourage, the mind and spirit to use the gift of *a go wa dv di,* vision—extraordinary ability to see beyond ordinary sight, to a better way.

There was a time . . . our wants were within our control . . . we saw nothing we could not get.
   SHARITARISH

July 12

The fragrances of the countryside are exhilarating after a summer rain. Wildflowers and morning glories have spread profusely along fencerows, and bittersweet vines abound wherever they can take hold. One breath of fresh air, one beautiful smell of petunias on the evening breeze, is never enough. It has to be repeated and held in remembrance for another time, another place. A pill doesn't exist that works better than a country lane after a rainshower. Huge drops make secret symbols in the dust and are *a da to li gi*, a blessing on the head of a Cherokee. It is a special message, a private baptism from the Great Spirit.

This country is mine, I was raised on it; my forefathers died on it; and I wish to remain on it.
CROW FEATHER

July 13

Summer heat has brought a lull to the meadows. Tiny titmice and bright yellow warblers stay close to watering places, and only the locust sings on in its raspy tones. It sings to remind us that it is summer and time to slow our pace. Hay meadows are dotted with bales, and wheat and beans are ready for harvest. Evening is alive with the songs of meadowlarks and killdeer, and the mockingbird is the comic that sings in all the other birds' voices. It would be impossible to live among the things of nature and not pace oneself to them. It is the nature of the Cherokee to go to a flowing stream with any problem he may have. And he comes away with the best harvest of all, a quiet eye and the peaceful harmony of summer.

I have a good heart, and I want no mistake made this time, to live with a good heart and talk truth.

CAPTAIN JACK

July 14

Never quit when the going gets rough. Now is the time to bear down even harder. It would be a shame to quit and find we had almost reached our goal. If a person that can't swim panics in deep water, he will sink. But if he rolls over and floats for awhile, he can get his sense of balance and make the distance easily. The Cherokee believes he can endure, he can work, and he can fight. He will not be *a tsv na*, turned back. We owe it to ourselves to see what we can accomplish. And it may well be that we can do what others said is not possible.

You showed me . . .the spirit shape of things as they should be. You have shown me, and I have seen.
BLACK ELK

July 15

A shallow river that is not deep enough to hold all the water that runs into it during the rainy season is always in danger of pushing out of its banks. When it overflows, everything is in danger. Those who live near such a river know they must be prepared. They have seen havoc wreaked on everything in its way. But they have the same feeling about people who are so like the river. Such people have no control and no depths, and tend to push into the lives of other persons. Many of the walls we build are to protect us from intrusion. The Cherokees remember that need for *a li s de lv to di,* safety or protection, and will not again be caught in the floodtide.

No man of my race has ever stood there before. The flood rises, looking upward I see a steep, stony path. I lead the way up . . . .
    STANDING BEAR

July 16

If time were a dollar—how careful we would be with how we spent it. We wouldn't spend it on worry, for we know fretting is not profitable. Anything limited makes us conscious of what we do with it, whether it is time or money or the people in our lives. How we value what we have decides what we keep. The Cherokee doesn't want many things, but they know the wise are *i yv da*, careful or mindful of what is important. Such caution teaches us to think before we talk, to slow our pace and find peace of mind. It eventually gives us more resources, and more time to enjoy them.

If we could have spared more, we would have given more . . .

CANASSATEGO

July 17

There is little wrong with the earth that it cannot clean up itself. It renews constantly, trying to keep pace with so much tampering going on. It has its hot spots, its upheavals, and the recycling of elements—but the Indian has known how to live with the changes. It is the world of people that needs to clean up its act. Some think the trouble began when the atom was split—but it was more apt to be when man split with the Great Holy Spirit. We learn from the earth not to build up too much pressure or we will blow it. The river has taught us we can't be too broadminded or we spread out in the shallows and dry up in the midday sun. When moral standards were lost in the shuffle, the world kicked over the lantern again.

Hear me, not for myself but for my people . . . that they may once more go back . . . and find the good road and the shielding tree.

BLACK ELK

July 18

Time is the supreme equalizer. It puts us on the same level with people that never considered us their equal. The person in most revered and feared position can suddenly have his breath taken away by sudden descent. Time seems almost mischievous in the way it turns things around. We never really know what people think or what they believe until they have had some time. Our only drawback is how we think about ourselves and the need to talk about it. When our mouths are talking, our minds stop to listen. We may not like what time has done—but we can rely on its fairness. It has seen our actions, heard us talk, and knows our hearts. We can only hope there is enough time that we can learn and change.

Like the wildwood birds which our fathers used to hold their breath to hear, they sing in concert . . . alike in forest and field . . . alike before wigwam or castle . . . alike.

POKAGON

July 19

It began at dusk, a walk along the edge of the alfalfa field, with a chorus of crickets and the soft rumble of thunder in the distance. A doe stood spellbound with curiosity. Motionless but ready for flight, she watched and waited. The ridges and ravines have not lost their beauty since our grandfathers hunted game and left their arrowheads for later generations. They walked here in the mist, and watched a break in the clouds shoot rose-red color to make rainbows—lovely muted colors with no defined edges. The reflections and subtle shadows hung on until dark snuffed them into a deep, blue haze. The land is wild and beautiful with ancient oaks that could testify to many events. The great horned owl could tell us how its hoot was mimicked by our grandfathers—and how it answered.

We will never let our hold to this land go . . . for it would be like throwing away . . (our) mother. . . that gave us birth.

AITOOWEYAH

July 20

The hours were longer when we were children. Summer was a time of sunlight, bare feet, and shade trees. We fished in a creek with a crooked pole and feasted on potatoes and onions cooked over an open fire, which the Cherokee calls *a tsi la*. It was a good time, and we expected everything to be good. There was time to daydream—or hide out in a secret place and be quiet. Now we have less time and more responsibility—or have we let fear steal our joy? If we let it, it will tell us we can't remember details, we hear less, our vision is blurred and we are afraid of what we see and read. Fear is a contaminate that dulls our senses. But it can't affect us when we turn around and renew and restore our minds. The creek and the sunperch are still there to help.

We sang songs that carried in their melodies all the sounds of nature—the running of waters, the sighing of winds, and the calls of the animals. Teach your children . . .

AMERICAN INDIAN

When we are appalled at the other person's ignorance, it is hard to believe that our own is just as profound. We stand in awe that they do not see what is so apparent, but in all our self-confidence we are as much in the dark as the next person. We are just ignorant on different subjects. What one person studies intensely may mean nothing to someone involved in another idea. But it takes all of us to make up the families of the world. We each have a purpose—and none of us quite like another. Time, circumstances, and beliefs have separated some as far as the east is from the west. It is not that we were created to be *nu da le hna v*, different or separated—but that we chose. We chose. We had the freedom to choose, and therein lies the difference.

You think I am a fool, but you are a greater fool than I am.

SITTING BULL

July 22

We are forever in transition—continually moving, changing direction, doing differently than we imagined. If we were to stop and analyze the past and what lies ahead, we would know that if anything is required of us, it is to be flexible. Not flexible in seeing everything one color, one ideal, one belief— but bending without breaking, able to see the chaos and not fall down under it. It is our duty, our *a da du da lv ne di*, obligation, to move and bend without creating a rift in our own spirit. A house cut in two cannot stand. However far we move in any direction, we must get it back together, we must bond with the law of our own spiritual being—which is to love others as we love ourselves. But we have to first love ourselves.

I had a dream . . . that the maker of all was Wakan tanka . . . to honor Him, I must honor his works.
    BRAVE BUFFALO

July 23

Much is lost through misunderstanding—and often because we want someone to know we are angry. We choose to think they intentionally displeased us, though we know nothing of their circumstance or what their thoughts really were. It must be an ego-building thing to believe that someone is trying to offend us. Somehow it gives an importance where there had been none. We have the uncanny knack of building a sad story with such realism that it makes us think we are more important than we are. It is not enjoyable to be the kind of person who wants to misunderstand—not only other people, but also life itself. It is painful to be unhappy and disagreeable, but some cannot resist the temptation.

It has come to me through the bushes that you are not united (agreeable); come to me when you are united.
    BIG BEAR

July 24

How like moths we are when we are caught in the dark, beating our wings against anything that stands between us and the light. Though we strain against barriers, we are the *a tsv s dv*, we are the light or candle that lights the place where we are. Others who follow watch for a signal, a light in the dark, to know they are not alone. We need to take some time to be quiet, to recharge and it may mean waiting a while in the dark. But whatever our need, if we wait the light will come. And it will illumine us instead of blinding us with its glare.

The path to glory is rough and many gloomy hours obscure it. May the Great Spirit shed light on yours
BLACK HAWK

July 25

The haying season is in full swing and trucks loaded with bales of green-gold leave the meadows stirred into action. Killdeer circle overhead, and quail call for a covey scattered by the noise of machines. To all appearances, this is the quiet season—but appearances are deceiving. The end is never the end but another beginning. The grasses drying in the sun have dropped seeds that will sprout again. Tall graceful sunflowers shade the wild petunias that wait for another rain. We finish one thing and begin another—always with a fresh eye for how we can do better. It reminds us that what we want to reap, we must first plant and cultivate and water with love.

The Great Spirit has smiled upon us and made us glad.

KEOKUK 1848

July 26

Ifwe squint our eyes a little when we look in the mirror, the result isn't so bad. But when we pass a mirror and catch a reflection unexpectedly, it reveals more than we wanted to see. In a brief moment, we caught ourselves unaware. There was no time to narrow the eyes—and there we were without a disguise. It was a stranger. No smiles—just grim. Why is it we think we are smiling when we are not? The Cherokee often has a stoic expression, *a du tiv to di*, a mask that protects his sensitive nature from the world around him. Others are the same way. It helps to have a sense of humor when we are caught off-guard.

Old Lakota knew that man's heart away from nature becomes hard.
STANDING BEAR

July 27

Perfectly intelligent people lose what they want most by demanding something that is still in the courting stage. There is a time to be bold, or *ni ga na ye s gv na,* says the Cherokee, but it takes wisdom to know when it is. If something is worth having, it is worth waiting for, worth working toward. But fear of losing something before we have had a chance to make it our own can stir us to take risks that are often unwise. Insecurity makes us react in plain-speaking ways that cause us to lose the very thing we want to keep. Action is a necessary part of living, but persuasion is an art and seldom appears demanding.

The Great Spirit will not punish us for what we do not know.

RED JACKET

233

July 28

Other people may tell us they know what is best for us. And maybe they do at times. But it is more important that we have time to know for ourselves what we are to do. The strength of other people tends to wane after awhile, so we need strength of our own to sustain us when no one else is around. Few stay prepared for any event. But we know to put our *go hi yu di*, our faith, where it helps us. When we get to those places of not knowing what to do, we shouldn't do anything—not until we have had time to stand still—and see.

The earth and myself are of one mind.
CHIEF JOSEPH

July 29

First impressions are reflections of what we are ready to think. How easy to believe we already know another person when we know ourselves so little. None of us reveal who we really are until we feel safe, and then it is a long time before we trust anyone enough to call them friend. We need to be told that we are liked—not once but many times, *ta li a le-yu go di-wo di s ge s di,* or "twice or more say it," is the way a Cherokee puts it. Even the most innocent of us tends to judge. But to judge before we know someone may show a lack of sincerity in our own makeup—or maybe even a little fear that we may see in others what we are afraid of finding in ourselves.

We concealed nothing. We came not secretly nor in the night. We came in open day.
MANGAS COLORADAS

July 30

Wetalk about choosing our friends, but true friends are self-selected. It is they who decide to respond and by what method. And finally they make themselves our friends by being loyal and having a genuine concern for our well being—or allowing privacy when it is needed. Acquaintances wait and judge. And sometimes it is better to be acquaintances when we cannot find a common ground on which to be friends. There is honesty in admitting we cannot be dear friends to all people. But there is always something special. A friend is a *unali*—without question or fear or concern for equal time. This is why friends are dear to us. They have chosen to be so.

The white man does not obey the Great Spirit; that is why the Indian never could agree with him.

FLYING HAWK

July 31

Rejoice when the going gets rough, when everything turns mean. It is time to shout and clap our hands—if only in the privacy of our own minds. To rejoice in difficulty doesn't seem reasonable, because the natural way would be to give up and cry. But we rebound from trouble faster when we turn off the tears and turn on the joy. It comes from the inside and goes to the outside—and that is how the *u hi so di*, the spell or gloom, is broken. If we have never done it before, we need to learn how to think joy and act joyful, because the heart is listening—and it is out of the heart that all issues are settled.

I beg you now to believe that, all miserable as we seem in your eyes, we consider ourselves nevertheless much happier than you.

GASPESIAN CHIEF 1676

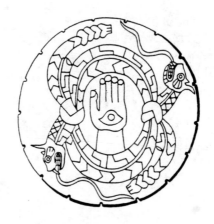

AUGUST

Galo'nee
End of Fruit Month

_Inclination to move from this land has
no abiding place in our hearts, and
when we move we shall move by the
course of nature to sleep under this
ground which the Great Spirit gave to
our ancestors and which now covers
them in their undisturbed repose._

CHIEF JOHN ROSS 1830

August 1

Going fishing to the Cherokee is *a na su hv s gv,* and it is never a waste of time. And neither is dawdling along, or staring into space. Great people have known the wisdom of taking time to let their minds drift with the cork on a fishing line. Who is to say that sitting quietly doesn't do more than running all over looking aggressive and building up blood pressure? Silence and down-deep thought can be just as active as making a big stir. Sometimes we learn something by study, but going fishing makes us wise. We know we can't sit still forever—but a little escape from the stress and pressure certainly makes a happier, healthier person.

Several of our young people . . . were instructed in all your sciences . . . but when they came back to us they were bad runners, ignorant of every means of living in the woods. . .
    SIX NATIONS

August 2

It is not easy to forget the hours we spent as children along some sparkling stream—and there were more sparkling streams then. It is not hard to remember every sound that carried up the creek, how the fishing was, and how it tasted fresh from the water and cooked in an old tin skillet over an open fire. There were *a tsi nv s gi*, violet flowers, blooming in clusters along the banks—and poison ivy we had to avoid—and didn't always. A cardinal sang a fishing song and the sound of oars dipped in warm water with a soft splish-splash. Bugs, like people on water-skis, slipped over the surface of water. And as we passed, *tsisdvna*, crawfish backed into holes in the mud. Every moment was a thing of joy and knocks softly on our minds today when the need for solitude is there.

What is life? It is the flash of a firefly in the night . . . the breath of a buffalo in the winter time . . . a little shadow which runs across the grass and loses itself in the sunset.

CROWFOOT 1821

August 3

Love and abuse are never compatible. When someone claims to love us regardless of how they treat us, we should take it with a grain of salt. It is the cry of someone who needs to lean more than to love. Need is a net thrown over a prey. It is the spider tightening the threads of its web to catch what it needs. Love doesn't threaten and intimidate one minute and practice persuasion and promises the next. Love is not just emotional words. It is the need to give and support and protect, even when comfort is threatened. It is not manipulation and it is never, never *u yo i gv ne di,* abuse.

A child believes that only the action of someone who is unfriendly can cause pain.
CHASED-BY-BEARS

August 4

Anytime we fall down in doing anything and we get up and have another go at it, count it all progress. It is getting up that makes a warrior, *di tli hi*, as the Cherokee says it. Getting up doesn't mean the warrior is fearless or that he is totally self-confident. It does mean that he gains confidence as he persistently keeps trying, and he fully expects strength to come as he needs it. He asks, *na quu na*? How about now? Everyone is afraid of a challenge, afraid of being down and staying down. But relying on the Great Spirit gives the courage to speak powerful words to bolster the human spirit. So, how about now?

I know the Great Spirit is looking down upon me from above, and will hear what I say . . .
SITTING BULL

August 5

It is strange how the same words spoken yesterday have a different meaning today. What can we say that we have not already said before? And what can be said that has not been said so many ways? Some words can be said any number of times and still be new. The Cherokee say, *Gv ge yu a*, I like you or I love you. I love you to the ultimate amount for one day. But it will not compare with tomorrow. Tomorrow brings its own container to be filled. As the sun rises and the moon sets, time moves swiftly, and the need to love and be loved never changes. It helps us appreciate the finer things, knowing our hours together are as beautiful as polished gems that never lose their glow and always retain their value.

I feel glad as the ponies do when the fresh green grass starts in the beginning of the year.
TEN BEARS

August 6

Nature is positive. When one part of it drops away and returns to the great continuum of life, new shoots, new sprouts of life stand nearby to complete the purpose. One season moves on so that another can take its place—but it is no more and no less important than the one before. It is inherent in nature to be positive—as it was in the beginning for human nature. But human nature was given the option of choosing good or bad. It chose to disobey, and now we know fear and anxiety. A Cherokee expression, *u so nv-i ya dv ne di*, calls this a wrong act, a misdeed, that brought about a longstanding situation that has to be dealt with more than we would like. But we have a choice as well, and we must consider who is standing alongside to be the new sprout to complete the purpose.

Great Spirit . . . To the center of the world you have taken me and showed me the goodness and the beauty and the strangeness of the greening earth . . . you have shown me, and I have seen.

BLACK ELK

August 7

The path through the woods has a light layer of scarlet leaves that have fallen early from the woodbine. Crickets are chirping the coming of a new season—and the sassy blue jay, *tla yv ga,* agrees. Touching the earth is a lovely feeling that once again we find our beginnings. Whether we walk or plant or plow, it is a place created for us, a place to stand with bare feet to feel comfort spread quietly through us. The pulse of the earth slows our own and tranquilizes confusion. Seeing the *ga lv lo i,* sky, in its limitless depths stirs us to imagine, to stretch our awareness to know how much beauty is provided for us. It helps us to see that mean things can only last as long as we allow them. Nothing can hem us in when we know the freedom of spirit.

I was born on the prairies where the wind blew free and there was nothing to break the light of the sun. I was born where there were no enclosures. . .

GERONIMO

247

August 8

Life is one long courtship of things we want or fear. Whether it is something we want or something we want to avoid, we *gu na da yi li da s di,* court it, woo it through our thoughts and words, reaching with intense effort. When our desires are too rigid, we have been known to create a psychological wall that shuts off the natural flow to carry out our heart's desire. We simply can't do what we want to do. When something is to be avoided at all costs, we tend to vision it so vividly that it has no choice but to come our way. The same mental law turns back what we want as well. We have to be careful about what we want, because we are apt to get it. It is our nature to court, but wisdom should always be there.

I ran to the spring to fetch water for them when they were thirsty. By these little services I won their affection . . .

PLAYFUL CALF

August 9

Tradition is a basic part of life. It provides a pattern on which we can depend to give us a sense of belonging, a security. But it can also be a block in the way of new progress and new learning. We owe it to ourselves to preserve *ka no he lv hi*, the old ways of life, the traditions. But we owe it to ourselves not to be so deeply conditioned to doing something the same way for so long that we stagnate for the sake of it. Too many of us sit on the fence, walk the middle of the road and keep our vision limited. It is not in our makeup to betray a tradition. But to break out of a mold in which we have been hand-pressed, to soar in our own right, is to be worth our salt—and worthy of all that has brought us this far.

In the Indian the spirit of the land is still vested; it will be until other men are able to divine and meet its rhythm.

STANDING BEAR

August 10

Warm August evenings afford us a view of the honey-slow movements of summer, *go gi,* in Cherokee. Cattle graze peacefully across meadows and the mockingbird that lives at the top of the mulberry tree sings the songs of other birds with great mimicry. The sky is streaked with vapor trails from jets still caught in the last rays of sunlight, just before a smudgy darkness settles over the horizon. Clouds, the kind an artist strives to paint, change colors before our eyes and sweep the western sky. It is the best time to escape the daytime heat and walk along the feed road that winds through the meadow. Tall sunflowers nod in a sudden cool breeze and the white fluff of milkweed carries across the fencerow. This is *to hi dv*—the peace—*u ne la nv hi,* the peace of God that passes all understanding.

Might I behold thee, Might I know thee, Might I consider thee, Might I understand thee, O Lord of the universe.

INCA SONG

August 11

At some point, all of us stand at a crucial fork in the road and decide which way we will go. When we stand firm in what we know is right, we can make the decision with confidence. We love that person who can stand at ease when everything threatens to go downhill. He not only looks like he can fight—which the Cherokee calls *a la s di,* but he is wearing an invisible armor of faith that makes him invincible. When we have chosen the right road and we are ready to do battle, a way is made where there has been no way. Our feet are set to go, and when we reach that crucial spot, we mark the road for those who follow.

Teach us the road to travel, and we will not depart from it forever.
    SATANK

August 12

Time and space mean nothing to friends. They find each other again and again, to share the things that are important—and a great many things that are ordinary, every-day events. *Tsu na li i*, friends or close ones, forgive us whether we deserve it or not. They know how easy it is to get off center. But they have high hopes for us—maybe even higher than we have for ourselves. We are at our best when someone chooses to be that kind of friend, to make allowances for our lapses of memory—for no other reason than precious, loyal friendship. It is a quiet, peaceful and dear relationship that never grows old and never ends. Being such a friend is a sweet and blessed responsibility.

The Great Spirit has smiled upon us and made us glad.

KEOKUK

August 13

There are right things to say and right ways of saying them, but many times we hit on a touchy subject because we were talking when we should have been listening. A casual remark that doesn't mean much to us can strike a nerve in someone else. Even when we disregard other people's feelings by saying they are too sensitive—it may be that we are too *ni ge ya ta hv na*—careless or callous. Over the years we may learn how to make friends and how to keep them—and most of it is done by controlling our tongues. No matter how close we are to someone, it does not give us the right to say anything we choose.

You must not hurt anybody or do harm to anyone.
WOVOKA

August 14

We have heard that all things come to those who wait—which may be true to some degree. But it seems more sensible that all things come to those who expect them, who get ready and work toward having them. Far too many wait for happiness to run them down and force joy on them. But having the right to something doesn't make it happen. Joy is like a bubbling spring that pushes its way up through layers that would keep it from flowing. And joy is the essence of life, the *s du i s di,* the key. When something is presented to us, we can't pick it apart and find fault with it. We don't look around and see if someone else is interested in it before we decide—but we take it by the hand and walk with it, learn about it, bless it, and find that we have waited long enough.

I fear no man, and I depend only on the Great Spirit.
KONDIARONK

August 15

Most people do not intend to get caught in a bad cause. We simply get swept along with the tide. It can happen because we want to get ahead fast—but it more likely happens out of ignorance. It has been said that we have the capacity to make heaven a hell, or a heaven of hell. We've been known to do both—though it is a matter of choice. According to the Cherokee, it is plain to see that the place called heaven, *ga lv la di-tso sv*, is the ultimate choice. We have had to deal with situations that we didn't choose. They were simply piled on us and we tried to help. But here we must be wise. We can't allow ourselves to be drawn into a cause that is not our responsibility, and that we may not be well informed enough to handle.

I have been trying to seize the promises which they made me . . . but I cannot find them.

BIG BEAR

August 16

Some people claim to have no need of solitude. Others insist on privacy, a time away from everything to get a better perspective. Most of us want our moments of quiet—but we want to decide when they are to be. We want the *u tse li dv* solitary hour as long as it has a spirit and aliveness. It is in the quiet times that we build our strengths and know we have something to rely on. Solitude is not withdrawal into a place where no one and no sound can penetrate. It is a sweet moment of peace with or without other people that lets us recenter and reset the rhythm of the mind, body and spirit. It is wisdom to stay close to the solitude of nature to keep us young and pliable.

Old Lakota was wise . . . he kept his youth close to its softening influence.
STANDING BEAR

August 17

We never really lose anyone. If they were ever a part of our lives, they are always a part of our lives. The important thing is not to regret what has gone before but to take from it the lesson, the experience that was in it for us. Life is a two-way street, not always sunshine and flowers but a few clouds, a few tears, go with it. It is a complex mixture of many things we are supposed to glean from it. We cannot park by what went wrong, nor can we linger forever by something we might have done right. It is a progressive, moving time filled with new experiences, memories both good and not so good, and many promising hours. It is possible to put our emotions aside and remember joy. But above all, the best is yet to be.

The Great Spirit placed me here. . . to take good care of the ground and to do each other no harm.
YOUNG CHIEF

August 18

I t takes enthusiasm to do anything. We go through so many of the same things day after day that we tend to lose our eagerness for some of it. But if we stir ourselves up, enthusiasm, like a primed pump, will flow more easily. When people lose their taste for life, it is not that there is no longer anything interesting— but they are no longer interested. They need to stir themselves up and get out of the doubting rut they have dug themselves into. The Cherokee associates the lack of enthusiasm with being sad, which he calls *u hi so di*. Enthusiasm has wonderful effects on the mind and body—giving them a chance to heal, to recover from unhappy experiences. When we lack enthusiam, let us say we have it—enough to do anything we have to do.

The Great Spirit smiled upon us and made us glad . . . but we had to agree . . .

KEOKUK

August 19

To live peacefully with other people, we need insight and careful judgment. We judge by appearances far too often and that leads to misunderstanding. So much is hidden from ordinary view that it takes time to know something well enough to say anything at all. We have to know that because we have light does not mean there is no darkness. And because we have food does not mean there is no hunger. Can our eyes see all the reasons and purposes in the actions of other people? Unless we have known someone's pain and carried his burden, we cannot know how we might react in the same circumstances. Our senses cannot tell us everything. Only compassion and understanding show us the truth.

O Great Spirit, help me never judge another until I have walked two weeks in his mocassins.

EDWIN LAUGHING FOX

August 20

We have taken many paths we would not have chosen, and we have done many jobs we did not want to do. We have carried burdens we did not want to carry and dealt with impossible people we did not like. It is strange that the road we did not want to take is the one that brought us more quickly to the place we wanted to be. At times, the way was hostile, but when we needed a hand there was one. When we needed courage, it was there. What we call problems and unjust circumstances have a way of teaching us integrity and how to be peaceful. It makes us wonder how many other rewards we have missed because we resisted something that looked like too much responsibility.

I was going around the world with the clouds when God spoke to my thought and told me to . . . be at peace with all.

COCHISE

August 21

Sometimes wisdom is knowing what to overlook. Often it is forgiveness without putting it in words. But why would any quick-thinking, industrious person of knowledge and intellect want to overlook anything? Because we never know when we are going to be in another person's shoes. If it should happen, we want to be forgiven—for a variety of reasons. Overlooking shortcomings is not just wisdom—it's kindness as well. Who has not hoped the world was looking the other way when he or she fell short of being admirable? To overlook in Cherokee is *a hi ya s to di*—meaning almost the same thing as to ignore. What a blessing to not be ignored, but to have our faults overlooked.

You must not hurt anybody or do harm to anyone.
You must not fight but do right always.

WOVOKA

August 22

Every time we think we make a mental picture. The more we look at the picture on the motion picture screen of our minds, the more real it becomes. We forget that it is imaginary, but our emotions pick up on what the mind has seen and the image causes delight, or tears, or even anger. Our emotions manipulate us and cause us to do things we would never do under different circumstances. When we give in, these mental suggestions cause us pain, jealously, and even anger. If our mental vision tells us we have been wronged, anger causes us to react foolishly. In such cases, we tend to go on the warpath, not for any commonsense reason, but because we fed ourselves the wrong mental pictures.

We do not take up the warpath without a just cause and honest purpose.

PUSHMATAHA

August 23

Painting a picture is much the same as living a life. Some of us only get the outline sketched while others find the time and desire to mix beautiful colors and brush them on canvas. Color is used sparingly on some canvases, others are somber and dark with little or no highlights. But those who use cheerful colors, cardinal reds, sunflower yellows, and all shades of purple and lilac, show us that life does not have to be ordinary. The Master Artist, *U ne la nv hi*, gave us all pallets and pots of bright colors to use boldly, or to mix in subtle but lively shades. We have been given the general sketch but it is left to us to fill in the colors, harmonizing and blending until we get the right tones. Each of us is a painter and each has the charge to make life a work of art.

They searched for a long period of time for the source of life, and at last came to the thought that it issues from an invisible creative power to which they applied the name Wa-ko-da.

PLAYFUL CALF

August 24

Nothing saves the day so much as a good word. And nothing has been misused as often. There is power in a word, whether we read it, speak it or hear it. And we command and are commanded by the word. We scatter, we call forth, and we comfort. Words are tools, weapons, both good and bad medicine—but very beautiful when used lovingly. The word, or *ka ne tsv* in Cherokee, is power to help heal, or make sick people sicker by negative talk around them. The word gives confidence when it builds rather than destroys. Relationships have been shattered beyond repair by a run-away mouth. Prosperity has been dissolved by talking lack. Until we listen to our own voices and how we talk, we would never guess how we use our words.

I am opening my heart to speak to you . . . open yours to receive my words.

COMO

August 25

We have a flair for convincing ourselves that there is nothing we can do about certain things—when it is more likely we don't want to do anything about them. As long as we still care enough, we go on looking for solutions and hoping for miracles. But every day that goes by distances us from so much that no longer stirs us. Gradually, those things we thought so important fade and slip out of our daily thought. It is called *gv ge wi s di* in Cherokee, and means neglect in anybody's language. It is one thing to let something go when it means nothing, and another to think we still have control and find the urgent need to retrieve it. What is important? It is vital to know what we want and need—if we are ever to have it.

I was very sorry when I found out that your intentions were good and entirely different from what I supposed they were.

SITTING BULL

August 26

It is comforting to know that every day we are in contact with people who put such confidence in us that we strive harder to do our best. These are the ones that build people and there's no job more fragile or creative than giving others confidence. No two people ever respond the same way, and since there can be very little trial and error in handling individuals, sensitivity to hurt and fear must be considered. Where one person can be challenged, another may need to be told how to rise above emotions and imagined short-comings. The Cherokee, like so many others, appears *u wo we la nv,* composed or stoic, but his nature is sensitive to criticism in any form. We all need approval and attention, and when someone cares, it makes an important difference.

That hand is not the color of your hand, but if I pierce it I shall feel pain. The blood that will follow from mine will be the same color as yours. The Great Spirit made us both.

STANDING BEAR

August 27

We might be able to go back and do things differently if we had new knowledge, new understanding. Otherwise, we would do the same things. We work with what we have, with what we know. To anguish over what we did in the past is foolish. If we intentionally did something that was wrong, it takes a little more handling—but most of our regrets are either imagined or history. It doesn't keep us from wishing we had been wiser and more careful—more able to see in the dark. The Cherokee calls this remembering the things that never were—*i ye li s di i*—over use of the imagination. On the other hand, it is the same thing that helps us see our way out of memories that tend to hold us.

He is no coward. Black Hawk is an Indian!
BLACK HAWK

August 28

Everything that thrives is fed by the light. Lift up a rock, and the seed that sprouted beneath it is bent, stunted and colorless. But after a few hours of filtered light it begins to straighten, and will eventually throw off all the effects of being held down. We need *a li so qui lv di,* a weight or a burden, lifted from our shoulders so we can grow and thrive in the light. We have to show willingness to stand on the rock and not beneath it. To see ourselves in better circumstances, to think clearly, is to be free. Little by little we see the possibility of health and order and great prosperity which includes everything we need. To see good and say good will eventually cause good, but our vision and our words must be steady.

You must speak straight so that your words may go as sunlight to our hearts.

COCHISE

August 29

To earn a standing place takes control, control of the tongue and all that leads to what it says. Being clever and having powerful connections is about as reliable as cheap scaffolding. It can all tumble down under the slightest pressure. Permanent security is never in things or in fame. Securing is an inner, personal reliance on what the Cherokee calls *Galun Lati*, or the Great Spirit. People have always attempted to amass fortunes and still be happy apart from anything spiritual. Things and fame can come to anyone willing to work for them—but contentment and health go hand in hand with the Great Spirit.

We never quarrel about the Great Spirit.
COCHISE

August 30

How can we know another man's heart or true desire? We're not even sure about our own. So many potent suggestions have been made to us that we question our own hearts. If we can understand who we are, we will know others. To identify something valuable in another person is to know it in ourselves. The *Tsalagi* calls it intuitive or perceptive—to know something without tangible evidence. The miracle is in finding something good in someone else and realizing we have to have it in us to be able to recognize it. One who never has a good word or a good thought for anyone reveals his terrible need.

Sentiment was against the Indian, that they could not be civilized . . . could not be educated . . . were somewhat like human beings. . . but not quite in line of human rights. . .

WASSAJA

August 31

The first thing we consider is how we feel—but feelings change on waves of emotion. As soon as we awake in the morning we test our feelings for how the day will go. It is like testing the wind for what day it is. Feeling and emotion are an important part of us—but only a part. If we give them power, they will *a s da wa dv s to di,* take over or rule us. How many times our emotions have caused us to be sick or to fight, when all we had to do was resist the suggestion. Our sensitivity to pain or hurt can make tears well up with self-pity and an even greater need to feed our emotions. When we have good reason to hurt, it will end sooner if it is allowed to go away.

We felt like talking to the ground, we loved it so, and some of the old men and women cried with joy when they reached their homes.

MANUELITO

SEPTEMBER

Dulu-stinee'
Nut Month

*When they sang, a line or two . . . of
a hymn printed in the Cherokee
language . . . I certainly never saw
any congregation engaged more
apparently in sincere devotion.*

GEORGE FEATHERSTONHAUGH

September 1

We may be physically bound to this earth, but we are eagles in our spirits. *Wo ha li,* an eagle, is the symbol of freedom with power to soar. Their nests are aeries built high above all other nests where nothing can touch their young. When *wo ha li* sets its wings to catch the wind, its flight is one of grace and beauty. *Wo ha li* takes time out to renew itself, to pull out old feathers so new ones can grow in. The eagle also removes portions of its beak and new growth replaces it. We can soar as well. Our spirits have no limitations and we can set our goals to any height we aspire to reach. When we set our minds and spirits to do something, nothing can bring us down except ourselves. But we do need to take time to rest and renew so that our flight is full and free right to the goal!

Your feet shall be as swift as forked lightning; your arm shall be as the thunderbolt, and your soul fearless.

METHOATASKE

September 2

Somewhere among our best times is a lost day. It was not lost all at once but minute by minute. It seemed only a moment of irritation or a few seconds of melancholy for no reason at all. But it all adds up to a day that gave nothing. The lost minutes are like the little foxes, the *tsu la*, that steal into the vineyard unnoticed to ruin the fruit on the vine. We take such care to keep out the bigger drain on our time, and let the little irritations, the times of melancholy and doubt steal our common sense and ruin the day. Life is so many little things, little ideas, little words—but combined, they are life. The only benefit is in recognizing that though we have lost a day, the remaining time can be lived without regret.

There was a time when our people covered the land as the waves of a wind-ruffled sea. . .that time long since passed. . . I will not mourn. . .
    SEATTLE

September 3

Every day we have choices. We may not like what they are, but we can choose how we will react. If we don't choose what we want in our lives, then life will decide for us. And if we do not like how it has chosen so far, we are sure not going to like what it has in the future. Few really think they have a choice. And it may appear that way—unless we are fighters. People willing to swim against the tide are fighters. They do not agree with everything they see and hear just to be one of the crowd. They think and act for themselves. We develop muscle when we swim upstream, and with the mental and spiritual power that comes with it, we accept and reject, change even the way we look—and find solutions we never knew existed.

Our eyes are opened so that we see clearly. Our ears are unstopped . . . for all these favors we thank the Great Spirit and him only.

RED JACKET

September 4

When we have an interest in something we seldom lack the energy to do it. We can keep at it hour after hour. But weariness follows routine and anything that lacks creativity and color. We can't always do what pleases us. There will surely be some necessary work that does not excite us—but all we have to do is refuse to be dull and unseeing. It shows in the way we walk and in our *i yu ni we dv*, our expressions. A sudden change from routine to something more exciting floods us with energy and a brightness that was there all the time. We just didn't know it and let feeling rule us. Energy flows when it is connected to a live circuit. Our work is to stay connected.

Rise to the dignity and grandeur of your honored position...shake off the base fetters of the bad spirit . . .
KEOKUK

September 5

Constant motion seems more important than waiting. But waiting is the time to prepare, to build up the spirit and be rested and ready. When anxiety grips us it uses up energy. It wastes our time. Waiting creates staying power so that there is no need to retreat, no need to go *a si ni,* as the Cherokee puts it, to go backward. Much depends on whether our waiting is a pause before going on, or an inertia that puts us in a trance. But when the mind, body, and spirit track together as a unit to move mountains, the waiting is only a prelude to action that makes up for any lost time.

The path to glory is rough and many gloomy hours obscure it.
  BLACK HAWK

September 6

The habitual comfort of a familiar place keeps us where we are—even when we are not happy there. The hurt of leaving something we have grown accustomed to makes it more difficult. It takes time to adjust—some say as much as six weeks. But once an adjustment is made, we could never go back. The ache for the old and familiar no longer has the pull it once had. Like the delicate tendrils of an ivy cling tenaciously, each sensitive feeling must be loosened and detached before we begin to feel at home. Until we lose the world we once knew, we cannot fully adjust to a new one. It is a slow, strange unraveling of old *a no da nv te s gv,* ways of thinking and doing. But one day we can look back and wonder why it took so long when being free and joyfully alive is so good.

While feeling compassion for you in the sweetness of our repose, we wonder at the anxieties and cares which you give yourself. . .
    GASPESIAN CHIEF

September 7

There are missing people in our lives. We don't know who all of them are because some have never been there. But there are voids that we know should have been filled. Our feelings go out and there is no one to send them back. Is it our fault? Did we do something that kept the place beside us vacant? The thought is painful because many others do not have such voids. They take for granted that there is a place for every person they need and every person is in his place. But the thought may occur to us that if we have empty places, then there must be someone out there with a vacancy because we are not there. We are the missing person in someone else's life. Do they *a da du hi s to di*, blame themselves because we are not there? They shouldn't, nor should we.

I cannot think we are useless or Usen (God) would not have created us. . . for each tribe. . . he made a home. . . and placed whatever was best for the welfare of that tribe.

GERONIMO

September 8

A change of season comes softly. Morning mists hang like gauze curtains through the valleys, and pockets of cooler air waft like thistledown on late summer breezes. The days are still warm with crickets trilling until rainshowers begin to cool the land. Even before there is credible evidence that fall is coming, one senses it in the air. The green willows bend gracefully in the changing wind and slowly change their color to sunshine. It is a time to enjoy what the Cherokee refers to as *ga ne tli yv s di,* the change-over, the freeing of the old season, the welcome to the new. It is the nut-gathering time—acorns, pecans, walnuts in abundance. The sweetness of the earth speaks to the feet and renews the spirit.

When I make peace, it is a long and lasting one.
    SANTANA

September 9

When we do something that falls below our best behavior, we give power to our worst enemy. And each time we overcome irritation and self-pity, we draw near our best friend. Our worst enemy, the Cherokee calls *adasgagi*, and our best friend, *unalii*, are one. They live in us and everywhere we go, they go. They speak to us, act through us, and vie for our attention. We are our own best friend and our own worst enemy. One is stronger than the other at times. But it is our decision which will rule and which one we will nurture, because we are the life and the strength of each one. Our lives, our health, and prosperity are all evidence of what we let rule us.

I am here by the will of the Great Spirit, and by his will I am a chief.
    SITTING BULL

September 10

There are exceptions to the rule—but generally speaking, nobody loves you like your mother loves you. Somewhere in the finely meshed fabric of life she wove a strength, a golden cord that ties you to her and releases you to go at the same time. The binding is not to possess but to protect, to be there when she is needed. In youth, we felt the strain of too much watchfulness, too many questions. But time, the equalizer, shows the quality of love was more unselfish than we thought, more precious than we ever dreamed it would be. And greatest of all, it is not blood that connects but simply a choosing to love because she wants to, not because of duty. It frees us to know that if we were chosen to be loved, then this must surely be the time to say, "*Gv ge yu a, U ni tsi.*" I like you, or I love you, Mama.

Comanche may die tomorrow, or ten years. When end come then they all be together again. I want to see my mother again.

QUANAH PARKER

September 11

Some people have the gift of persuasion. It just seems their words ring more true than anyone else's. It may be the manner, the quiet confidence in which they speak that makes them more trusted and more heard than most. They can calm us or stir our emotions—sometimes in the wrong way. We put our trust in the authority of other people at a time when we should sort things out for ourselves. Who are these people with *u la ni gv gv*, with power in their words to test our strength? It would be a shame to listen to double talk when our great need is courage and quiet peace. The same power is on our tongues to build or short-circuit—other people and ourselves as well.

Today is fair. Tomorrow may be overcast with clouds. My words are like the stars that never change.

SEATTLE

September 12

Some things never fade or wither in the late summer sun. Totally adapted to heat and dry weather, the sunflowers grow tall and heavy with bright yellow blooms. They color the roadsides and fencerows with the first look of autumn. Quail abound in the meadows, nervously breaking cover at the slightest sound. But cooler, damper weather will make them covey up and hold tight when a quiet walker eases by pretending they are well hidden—*gv s ga lv* in Cherokee. As evening settles in, a spider is silhouetted against the sun's last glow—back and forth, a live shuttle weaving gossamer threads into an intricate design to catch a flying insect. It is a part of the serenity that pervades the silent hour before dark and sings a song: Peace be with you.

Tribe follows tribe, and nation follows nation like the waves of the sea. It is the order of nature, and regret is useless.

SEATTLE

September 13

Can any good thing come out of a mouth that cannot talk without complaining—and never has a good thing to say about anyone? Negative talk sets us up to lose. Even when down-talking is for effect, it is devastating. Words are alive. They shoot out like boomerangs and turn back to lift us up or flatten us with a painful thud. Nothing reveals the inner status of a person like talk. The person may look like an angel, but if the words are rotten, there is no flower garden there. People damn their lives out of habit. Like an unconscious *sasa*, goose, in a wheat field, they gabble without one thought. But the minute their well-being is challenged they ask what they did to deserve it.

There was a time when I had a choice . . .
    RED EAGLE

September 14

If we would all stop at once to pray for the children of this world, there would be change like none we have ever seen. So few children still have the right to be innocent. They are made to look like miniature adults, taught to act adult, and abused because of it. How tempted we are to sympathize and say that this is the way the world is, so what can we do? It lets us go on our way wishing things were different but doing nothing to make it so. Why? Because we have cut loose from our responsibility to *a da to li s to di*, pray. Where did we go wrong? We made children compete and gave them no inner-strength. We curled their hair and twisted their minds. We educated them but did not give them wisdom. But then, what can we do for them if we have not learned ourselves?

Are not women and children more timid than men?
    TONKAHASKA

September 15

There are echoes of many things past within each of us. Voices, sounds, thoughts—and only a few that ring clear as the chimes in a clock from many seasons ago. They call us back in persistent flashes of memory, demanding that we recall details, some of them best forgotten. Why do we hear echoes? Perhaps to clarify our feelings, to help us be objective about the present time so that we can correct or delete certain things from our lives. Like the well-fed *gi li* (dog) turns primitive at the sight of a bone, we sometimes pick up on our own instincts and react before we think. As long as we can adjust and begin to understand our emotional ties, we can understand how others feel and not make them pay for what we hear in our echoes.

I was born upon the prairie, where the wind blew free, and there was nothing to break the light of the sun.

TEN BEARS

September 16

There are many days when everything in the world stands taller than we do. It leaves us with a feeling of inadequacy, a notion that no matter what we do, others can do it better. But we can't give up here. Other people are on their path, and we are on ours. Fair comparisons cannot be made—not even by those who claim to be experts. Only time—*a li yi li sv*—shows who has what it takes to handle life well. It is just that some days take more out of us than others. And sometimes we take more than we give. Life and circumstances balance when we are not so intent on counting only what goes wrong. When we take the responsibility for ourselves and begin to live instead of waiting for a time to be happy—then we will stand taller than the world.

The white men and Indians kept fighting each other backward and forward, and then I came in and made peace myself.

SANTANA

September 17

The winner carries with him the quiet knowledge that though he has heard every argument, faced every opponent, felt every criticism, there is no turning back and no accepting defeat. Telling a winner that something is impossible is waving a red flag, a *ga da ti*. He insists on going ahead, persisting until what he is doing is so well-known to him that there is nothing left to do but win. Every winner knows in his heart that he is not alone. His spirit and his dream merge so that even a loss would only be a delay. What we put into an idea, what we dream it can be, what we believe for and work toward is likely to make it take shape.

In my early days I was eager to learn and to do things, and therefore I learned quickly.
    SITTING BULL

September 18

The biggest mountain is made of tiny grains of sand. The swiftest, deepest river consists of tiny drops of water, and in the swell of human existence, one of us is just as important as another. One little drop of water is as complete in itself as the whole *u we yv* (river) or the whole *a me quo hi* (sea). Even in the smallest way, we are just as complete and miraculous as any smart invention on earth. Many small parts make up the great, but each thing, each part, is infinitely important and necessary. We should never say we are not important. We are each essential, we have a definite purpose, and it is a sacred responsibility to develop and use what we have at hand.

I am not a child. I can think for myself. No man can think for me.

CHIEF JOSEPH

September 19

We learn early in life that it is painful to love. Caring about anything is a great joy, but it makes us vulnerable to heartache, and our emotions are nearer the surface. Our feelings are mixed because we want to shout to the whole world that we love and it makes us feel wonderful. It makes us feel superior, able to cope with things that once got us down. Suddenly, everyone is a friend and no one is left out of our circle of love—*a da ge yu di*. Some part of us wants to hide what we feel so as not to shine too bright or be too enthusiastic. We need a little reserve of self so that we don't deplete that part of us that generates life in us on a daily basis. But for whatever pain that may go along with caring—we would not give it up for anything.

Tell them how we loved all that was beautiful.

AMERICAN INDIAN

September 20

Touching the earth is resting on the breast of our mother. It is once again finding our beginnings—a knowing that this place where we stand or walk or plow or plant, is something created for us. We know it because the pulse of the earth slows our own and tranquilizes our confusion. Seeing the sky in all its limitless depths stirs our imaginations and stretches our awareness of the simple beauty provided for us. We can see that it is wrong to be bitter and know that it lasts only as long as we let it. When we reach toward the ceiling of our minds, we are as unlimited as the sky. As currents of air stir the fragrance of the flowers, we may not be able to see where it comes from but we sense its influence. Life is ours to enjoy as individuals and it comes from the Great Holy Spirit.

We sang songs that carried in their melodies all the sounds of nature . . .

AMERICAN INDIAN

September 21

C an there be anything more beautiful than the seasons of a tree? A tree stands in beauty from year to year and keeps its grace and dignity. Its secrets are at its center and it tells nothing of people and their passing events. We learn when we watch a tree. It constantly prunes itself, continually sheds any excess. When it is growing in a difficult place it sends down deep roots to grapple for a firm footing. Every leaf is unique and beautiful—but also they serve to remove toxic poisons from the atmosphere, and send out a clean fragrance to shade us from heat. To sit beneath a tree, or to lie on the earth beneath an oak is the essence of pleasure. But to see the topmost leaves that no human hand has ever touched is to see a common miracle—a miracle with a message that says to get a firm footing in everything that is good and stand tall with our eye on the sky.

It may be that some little root of the sacred tree still lives.

BLACK ELK

September 22

Like attracts like. If we give up, so will others. If we cry, so will they. But if we decide this is a new beginning, others will take courage. We influence other people. Our attitudes send out ripples of feeling—like the scent of flowers that floats on air currents. What we think and say sets the stage for what is to happen. We can change our minds, our words, our attitudes, and we stop crying. We act like our prayers are already answered and take steps to show we believe it. When the early morning sun breaks through the far side of the woods, the dark places are lighted and much healing takes place. And so it is with us.

Great Spirit, you lived first, and you are older than all need.

BLACK ELK

September 23

I t is the right of every person to see that all the important and precious things of life are not blown away like vapor trails in high wind. Promises are tossed off so that the word, once thought a contract, is only talk and not sincere. Are agreements and promises only for the moment and not to be kept? Another person's word is of no concern if our own integrity has grown thin. True friendship takes two. Envy and getting the edge is not being a friend. It is self-interest—and self-destruction. Do we expect others to be what we cannot be?

The wildwood birds . . . sang in concert, without pride, without envy, without jealousy . . .
    POKAGON

September 24

Too much time is spent trying to be something that has no substance. If a garden is planted in rocky soil, the seeds may germinate but the plants will die because they have no root system—no place to put down their feet. It is better to be the pillar than it is to tie all our hopes and aims to a piece of artificial scenery that blows over in the wind. What appears to be solid and dependable should be examined. A two-faced person should be looked at twice. What to rely on depends on what we think is important. Who do we go to when something troubles us? What is in the heart—and what have we planted to get a harvest? Invisible things have more to them than most things we see in the world.

The Black Hills are the house of gold for our Indians. We watch it to get rich.

LITTLE BEAR

September 25

When we were young we had to ask permission to do everything that made us happy. We still want permission to be happy. The child in us wants to be a happy adult, but there's no one to tell us we may. Have we ever been freed to give permission to ourselves? Can we be at liberty to follow tradition and still be an individual? Can we resemble a parent but be free to improve? Do we have permission to outlive, outdo, outwork all those who went before us? Too many feel they must adhere to their roots rather than having admiration and respect for them. Instead of being caretakers of the past and feeling we must have their illnesses, live a certain number of years, and say what was good enough for them is good enough for us—we can give ourselves permission to build on their foundations. It breaks the chains for them as well as for us.

To us the ashes of our ancestors are sacred . . .
SEATTLE

September 26

L ate evening is a good time to walk down the field road where cows graze on tufts of new green grass. Late rains have brought new growth to the meadows and wild flowers are coloring the slopes and soft, rolling hills. Field sparrows talk about intruders and a killdeer cries for attention so she can lead us away from her second brood. The voice of the redbird, *tojuhwa*, calls to its mate somewhere in the deep woods. This time brings to remembrance things gone by and the shape of things to come. It is peaceful, prayerful, and personal. Even the sunset that spreads rouge across the horizon is a reflection of heart and soul. It is a joy, a feast of days, a high point of life, a quiet moment when rest is needed.

Earth and the great weather move me. . . have carried me away. . . and move my inward parts with joy.
    UVAVUK, ESKIMO

September 27

We have power we have never used. But we live by sight and not by faith that anything could be different. The power to enliven ourselves waits to be used. It is the same power we used as children to see what we wanted rather than what we did not have. Inside every overweight body is a slim figure that waits to be free. Inside every person who claims to be broke is the need for quality and not quantity. Health and vigor are in the one who ails but something is trying to steal them. We cannot whip what we cannot recognize. Symptoms are not the problem. They are only evidence of it. The roots go deeper than surface remedies. The spirit knows but it is never consulted. The real of us is the spirit, but it has been over-ruled by the physical and mental.

Day and night cannot dwell together.

SEATTLE

September 28

Newborn babies can't walk or talk or focus their eyes too well. Ability comes with time. The baby calf in the field that was so strange looking and unsteady on its feet was running within the hour. The effort put forth to move gives strength to do it—and moves us to more effort. But like the tide, the effort to move is followed by a rest, and then movement again. Each effort makes the next time a little easier until there is maximum strength or full growth. Some things challenge our very existence. It is the nature of things. But every effort we make weakens the challenge. If we will not give up, but we move and rest, move and rest, the breakthrough comes, the power to overshadow and shrink a test.

Whatever the gains, whatever the loss, they are yours.
FIVE WOUNDS

September 29

Excuses rob us. If an idea is a good idea, it deserves a second look. If the need for a quick profit is more important than long-term success, then an idea that costs money and takes time to develop is probably not a good idea. The world doesn't want to wait. The fast dollar, the quick thrill, the big wind. It all falls down. The best idea of all is that if we want to do something and do it well, we shouldn't let the world know. We should keep our *di ni s go li* (heads) down, the *a ho li (mouth)* shut, and everything else in high gear. Where we put our faith makes all the difference.

I looked for the benefits, which would last forever, and my face shines with joy . . .

TEN BEARS

303

September 30

Peace like a river. Think it, feel it, see it flow in smooth currents that will not toss the smallest boat. Stress can raise the blood pressure. It can make our ears roar and our hearts race with panic. Stop, and say, "Peace. Be still." This has always worked to calm the storms. Some people need stress to feel they are competing successfully. Instead of quietly doing good work, they *a di sv s di,* scuffle or wrestle with imagined competitors and hidden foes. Stress is holding rigid opinions, but peace, *to hi dv,* is a river with the power to make energy enough to push a city—or heal a body.

Our hearts rejoice in the goodness of our Creator in having . . . united the heart and hand of the red man in peace.

JOHN ROSS

OCTOBER

Duna Na-Dee'
Harvest Month

Where we will find another home I cannot say, but I still intend to go back to the Nation, but whether there will be peace, safety and pleasure living there for a long time to come is doubtful.

Mrs. Willim P. Ross
A Refuge in Kansas, 1863

October 1

The breathtaking skies of October are vivid strokes of rose-gold and muted shades of lavender and deep purple. It is a show of light and color. Without an awareness of time, the sky changes with colors melting and running together, lifting and glowing as the sun drops farther over the horizon. The path is a misty, blue haze that turns to darkness beneath the trees. A glow from the sky lights the way for swifts in their pursuit of late-evening insects. Like the dimly-lighted theater after the play is over, this is often the best part of the show. Somewhere deep in the woods, an owl calls and another answers. A doe feeds on new blades of winter wheat, and peace settles over the land and in the heart, an evening reverie.

For more than seventy years I have hunted in this grove and fished in this stream, and for many years I have worshipped this ground.

SENACHWINE

October 2

The simple things of life are best. An hour of sweet solitude, a cluster of bright yellow mums, the call of quail in the meadow. It doesn't take much to please us. One elusive goal after another makes us hurry by some beautiful times. It seems autumn will stand still while we do other things. The trees lose their colorful leaves and they are no less pretty, but to see them in all their phases is even better. Certain things are required of us because to give and receive is the order of life—but it is the quiet, timeless, natural activity that rests us and glows in our faces. Everything is not duty. Some of it is reward, rewards we don't remember earning.

Today is fair. Tomorrow it may be overcast with clouds. My words are like the stars that never change.
SEATTLE

October 3

Need motivates us. Our lack of self-approval spurs us to look for it in others. How they think is important to us, because we are one of many who needs a chance to belong. It may never have occurred to us that we have told them what to think by our actions. Our worth is not measured by what someone else thinks–but what we think. One hour of self-approval does more for us than years of waiting to hear that we measure up. *U na to tsa li,* belonging, means being a respected member of the tribe, holding one's own in any situation. The Cherokee does it by being honorable, by honing skills, and by taking care of his responsibility to the tribe as a whole. It gives him a unique position and self-respect that comes in no other way.

If a man loses anything and goes back and looks carefully for it he will find it . . .
    SITTING BULL

October 4

We cry because we feel unhappy and unloved. We cry because we care. We cry because we hurt, but more than that, we cry because we are unwise. These are the tears that make more tears. Enough *di ga sa wo s di!* Enough tears! Most of the time we try to have as few tears as possible, but they are as much a part of us as laughter. They can do a cleaning job that nothing else can touch. But like everything else, it can be overdone. Emotional people are usually caring. And it either makes life worthwhile or keeps it in such upheaval that nothing can be positive. There is a time to laugh and a time to cry. We have to remember that enough is enough and try to balance our approach to living.

I heard . . . that I should be like a man without a country. I shed tears.

LITTLE WOUND

October 5

Dozens of experts are ready to tell you what cannot be done. The difference is in the person doing it. It isn't a matter of trying harder or giving more. Frequently, something doesn't click into place until we turn it loose and walk away. The release is not to accept defeat but it is saying we have done what we can and now we will stand and let it work. Mental and spiritual work continues—even after we relax. The mind will try to take over but can be brought into line by the spirit, which is most important from start to finish. It furnishes the wisdom, the gratitude, the connection with *U ne la nv hi* Who made all things.

The Great Spirit put it in the right place.

ARAPOOISH

October 6

Think for a moment of beautiful things–a bouquet of zinnias, red, yellow, and lilac. Think of laughing brown eyes and a vapor trail in a rose-colored sunset. Think of puppies rolling and tumbling on the grass and the laughter of children at play. See in your mind's eye the brilliant skyline of the city at night– think of good books, excellent music, a warm friendly smile, and hot apple cobbler with thick cream. Think of lovely things you may have forgotten–the *si gi gi,* the katydid singing in the night, a full moon glistening on crystal clear water, cheerful voices, happy prayers. When we think of these things it makes us have faith, *u wo hi yu ha,* that we will have them again.

Why do you ask us to leave the rivers, and the sun, and the wind, and live in houses?

TEN BEARS

October 7

Singing cures a world of wrong. We have learned to sing about everything–and some of it has caused better understanding. Singing with other people teaches us harmony, and listening brings out feeling and emotion. But *na ni we a* alone expresses more deeply what we have not allowed ourselves to feel. We can sing when everything threatens, sing to be serene, sing to overcome our fears. But the best is to sing with joy, *na ni we a*. Singing is infinitely better than yelling. It gives young and old a feeling of security–if not of amusement. Anyone can do it. Everyone should experience what a difference singing makes.

Give ear. I am the mouth of my nation. When you listen to me, you listen to all Iroquois. There is no evil in my heart. My song is a song of peace.
    KIOSATON

October 8

Mark Twain said he never let his schooling interfere with his education. Nor should we. Education is not a degree or a result of money. It comes from sifting experience for wisdom and knowledge. It shows in how we communicate it to other people. Sequoyah was an illiterate Cherokee genius. He learned the white man had ways of preserving his thoughts on paper, and from the depths of his own mind and spirit, he made a whole tribe literate by perfecting a syllabary—*ti ga lo qua s to di*—to help the Cherokee advance quickly. One man's love and wisdom gave him insight to open the minds of his people so they could write, read the Scriptures, and learn the marvels of Greek, Latin, and calculus. He called it the "talking leaf." But he gave us more than that—he gave us impetus to search our own minds for gems from the Great Spirit.

It is my wish and the wishes of my people to live peaceably and quietly with you and yours.

CORNPLANTER

October 9

Hope is our most constant companion. We hope the pattern of things will change for the better. Even in dire circumstances hope remains when all else seems to abandon us. But even then it is a thread strong enough to hold life together. Like a cork on a net, hope keeps us from sinking in our own fears. It helps us picture the way things ought to be so we can bring them about. We cannot say anything is hopeless when so much depends on our seeing beyond barriers. Hope is a part of our natural existence. With it the door is always open. Without it, even dreams tend to perish.

Now I can eat well, sleep well, and be glad. I can go everywhere with good feeling.

GERONIMO

October 10

Jealousy is never hidden. It seeps into conversation, shows in the turn of the head, lives on the tip of the tongue. Unbearable in any situation, jealousy wrings the noses of so-called competition and wreaks havoc in relationships. It is totally ignorant of the fact that we have to go within ourselves for the things that lift or lower us. What belongs to each of us has nothing to do with anyone else. To be *a dv yu go di*, jealous, is to be miserable. If we can't hold our own, we can go home and get ready and come back. But to have animosity toward everyone who threatens cannot cultivate good in anything.

While the Indians received us as friends, and listened with kind attention to our propositions, we were painfully aware of their lack of confidence in the pledge of the Government.

PRESIDENTIAL COMMISSION

October 11

Flowers and people have many similarities. The shy violets that take to the shadows to bloom in dewy quietness are so different from the bright yellow jonquils that dance in the sunlight. And then there's the beauty of the rose. It blooms in lovely colors, *di ka no di,* and has a fragrance all its own. But it must be handled gingerly or its thorns will snag like crazy. And the petunia. It grows anywhere, in any kind of weather, with very little attention. It is prolific, coming in many colors and scents the evening air with happy memories. Where do we see ourselves? Sometimes we are simply weeds–but even weeds flower and give us insight into our own natures.

My people resemble the scattering trees of a storm-swept plain . . .
SEATTLE

October 12

We have heard the unforgettable cries of snow geese on their way to warmer places. Long check marks in the sky that turn and glint in the sun like silver flecks, thrill us with their ancient ritual. When the season begins to change, nature gives us a new view of creation—a creation in which we are not alien. We were never an afterthought. This was prepared for us the same way we provide everything a newborn needs before it arrives. Our seasons can be renewed as well. But it is our decision, because we have freedom of choice. We are not programmed by nature. The Great Spirit gave us life and the wisdom to maintain it—and to enjoy it as well.

Each man is good in his sight. It is not necessary for eagles to be crows.
    SITTING BULL

October 13

Early autumn mornings are cocooned in low-flying fog so that even the birds are cautious in their flight. Clusters of rose-colored grasses are draped in dew-laden webs, and all along the path, silken remnants shimmer with the most intricate designs. For a few hours, the morning is softly hung with gossamer. Some of the webs are already in the process of being repaired where a leaf or a twig broke through. Each web has the mark of a special spinner, silver with pearly droplets in the mist, and transparent in sunlight. Surely, this would be sweet, *u ga na s dv,* to the tartest spirit. It not only paces the heart but lightens the load.

The Great Spirit . . . . made it to always change . . . sunlight to play. . . night to sleep . . . everything good.
FLYING HAWK

October 14

It is peculiar how important something can be at one time and how totally unimportant at another. As we grow, our interests grow. We lose sight of situations we thought to be footed in concrete. Lovely or unlovely, nothing stays the same. It cannot. It grows into something newer and better, or it gives way where it is. Life is a living, moving force at every moment. We would not have that change—but to live happily, we must change. We cannot allow ourselves to crystallize until we are inflexible. There is too much to shatter us if we cannot bend. To enjoy the present moment is to have the innate knowledge that the next one and the next can be even better.

My forefathers were warriors. Their son is a warrior. From them I take my existence, from my tribe I take nothing. I am the maker of my own fortune.

TECUMSEH

October 15

Down in the edge of the woods a grapevine swings back and forth in the dappled sunlight. Two squirrels, young ones, spend time swinging on the vine, chasing each other up and down and crossing from tree to tree. Their obvious joy in simply being alive is good to watch. We seldom do anything with great joy. Most of us are animated only when it serves a purpose—not a genuine enthusiasm. We are too full of ifs and oughts to find reasons to rejoice. Sometimes a change can jar us into an awareness of life, and that life is intended to be much simpler than what we make it. Now we are in a season of mellow breezes and a slower pace. If only we can move out of fear and be able to enjoy life minute by minute.

Your children wish to refresh your memory. They think you have forgotten the promises made them.

CHIEFS AND WARRIORS, OTTAWAN AND CHIPPEWAS

October 16

There is a certain degree of sameness in your life and mine...a sameness that says no matter how different we are...we can still identify with each other's daily problems and hopes and aspirations. You may have that basic quality of serenity and quiet confidence...and I of frivolity and eagerness... but we can still communicate through our basic sameness and through friendship, or *o li i*, as we Cherokees call it. If there is any greatness or strength in either of us, it will be from the standpoint of our consideration for each other and our understanding of unspoken concerns and the need for support. . . for the thread of sameness is from the Great Spirit that touches not only us but all with whom we are in contact . . . a silent bond that makes us one in courage.

Friend and brother: It was the will of the Great Spirit that we should meet together this day.

RED JACKET

October 17

No one is so destined to lose that he cannot turn the tide–if he wants to change. Overcoming requires us to put our shoulder to the wheel in ways we would not have considered in earlier times. We are greatly influenced by our beliefs about ourselves and whether we are supposed to win or lose. The Great Spirit always wants us to win. It is our indecisiveness that keeps things wavering. There is nothing wrong with winning–and believing we can is a good thing. The question, *a dv dv hv s gi*, is not of the Spirit-Creator, but of us. Love wraps us around with peace and healing, with eagerness to do great things. But we have to free ourselves to do it.

Brother, you say there is one way to worship and serve the Great Spirit. If there is but one Religion, why do you. . . differ so much about it?

As-go-ye-wat-ha

October 18

Friends are those who forgive you–they have to if they are going to be friends. It is there somewhere among all the unwritten laws that a friend is someone you can rely on when there's no word, no kept promise, no outward sign of *ali i,* which is friendship to the Cherokee. We can forget a friend's birthday–and we can't say that about anyone else. We can tell them our deepest, darkest thoughts and they will take us to lunch. We may mistake them as our keeper–but we never, never mistake them for someone ordinary. The hardest lesson we have to learn is that everyone is not a friend. Not everyone sees us as a child at times, needing support and comfort. But a friend sees all and says nothing–until the right time. And even then we are forgiven.

Waupaypay and I in those days called each other brother-friend. It was a life and death vow; what one does the other must do. . .
    RAIN-IN-THE-FACE

October 19

Today may be a turning point. It happens that way—not with flashing lights and fanfare, but quietly. In the past we searched for reasons, for something we could pinpoint as the catalyst for change. We could never decide what it was, though we said many things. Something in us, something about our awareness, gives us reason to suddenly be conscious of new circumstances and new ideas. We are able to think outside the limits of our usual methods. Life, for no apparent reason, begins to fit together as though we found a piece of the puzzle that completes the picture. As turning points go, some are not particularly great to see, but are often hidden in such small, ordinary events as to go undetected. Our part is to be aware of the change and make the most of it while it is at its strongest.

The land . . . belongs to the first who sits down on his blanket . . . which he has thrown down on the ground, and till he leaves it, no other has a right.

Tecumseh

October 20

The crickets know that summer is over. They hide in tall grasses to see-saw out an autumn tune. No longer spry in the legs, one of them staggers out of hiding, to crawl over a grasshopper that has already sung its finale. Amid the changes, long-awaited rains bring out an abundance of sunflowers, spikes of pink thistles and the purple plumes of elegant blazing star. It is a rebirth of an earlier blooming season when there was less time to enjoy it. Cooler air brings out the elusive doe with her half-grown fawn to feed in the fescue field. Raccoons leave tiny handprints on the moist earth around the pond, and 'possums make a beeline to the persimmon trees. Watching the new season come in with such peace is a *da na li s da yv hu s gv*–feast for the soul.

The islands in the Mississippi were our gardens, where the Great Spirit caused berries, plums and other fruits to grow in abundance. . .
   BLACK HAWK

October 21

We live with memories. Every day, in some way or other, we are influenced by something or someone from the past. A deep reservoir of feelings and emotions make us dedicated to preserve some of what was and is important and *u wo du hi*, beautiful. But this is a new day in which to renew. We have a purpose or we wouldn't be here. Part of it is to make every hour count. We can't kill time without hurting ourselves, without wasting something very precious. Events that leave us drained may be to put us in line to take hold of a whole new way of life. Life will not destroy the memories but will preserve them to serve as a foundation for greater things to come.

If the Great Spirit has chosen anyone to be the chief of this country it is myself.

SITTING BULL

October 22

In the rush of deadlines, we forget to be glad for all the things that go right. But when one thing goes wrong, the counting starts. Before the day ends, we know exactly how many times we have been put upon. Anything out of order that gets our attention, *a ga se s to di,* in Cherokee. We ask, What next? And before we know it we are programmed to respond only to negative incidents. The day goes better when we decide early on that if anything can go right, it will. It keeps us looking for order rather than disorder—and that which the eyes of our mind are fastened on will respond.

The soldiers. . . never explained to the Government when an Indian was wronged, but reported the misdeeds of the Indians.

GERONIMO

October 23

Courage is like muscle, it doesn't develop to full capacity until it is used. Courage comes when we stir it up in our spirits and refuse to look at the shape things are in or believe there is nothing we can do about it. Most of us are timid about facing up to what we know is wrong. It is so much easier to let things ride than it is to take a thorny problem by the smooth handle and shake out the causes. To have courage doesn't mean we have to be aggressive and show everyone we are not afraid. Some of the bravest men in history were Indian chiefs trying to protect their land and their people. They used their skills in speaking to bring understanding.

My friends, your people have both intellect and heart; you use these. . . in what way you can do the best to live. My people. . . are precisely the same.

SPOTTED TAIL

October 24

As children we were taught that if we couldn't say something good, we shouldn't speak at all. Children should be taught the same thing now, and adults should remember what they learned. To keep a gentle tongue is a constant challenge. There are so many things to speak our minds about–though it might not be heard in the din of other voices. Wherever a dominant personality runs on verbal destruction, there's not going to be any peace. The Cherokee calls this chaos a *e hi s dv,* a pain or an ache or a headache. It keeps everyone feeling just bad enough that they can't give their best. Where there is hassle and harassment, there can be no constructive work. There will be nothing achieved without a gentle tongue.

We took an oath not to do any wrong to each other or to scheme against each other.

GERONIMO

October 25

A rainy day has such charm with its soft shadows and mist that hangs in the woods. The restful sound of rain on the roof and the way it sings in the downspout is reason to relax. The path to the woods is carpeted with yellow leaves and a few red ones washed down by the rain. Robins strut around like old-time preachers in tails. They love the rain because the ground is softer and they can feed without working so hard. On a restless day when the sun is too bright and there are too many noises, lie back and listen to a memory–listen to the *a ga s gv* patter on the roof and feel the peace that it brings. A good memory is as effective as the rain that caused it.

Fathers, our hearts are good . . . when we are at peace . . . we sleep easy . . .
SPOTTED TAIL

October 26

Misunderstanding is as contagious as measles–it moves from person to person, skipping only those who have developed an immunity. When there is an outbreak of misunderstanding in one place, there will be others–and not necessarily related. The source is usually a personality under pressure and the vibrations are felt like rumbling before an explosion. It is not necessary to get caught in cloudy issues. If we hear something we can refuse to pass it on. This is what happens when someone half listens but tells what he heard with little variations. When we keep our own opinions and refuse to be drawn into double-talk, our conscience is clear and we have not sent out anything to come back to us when we least need it.

I speak straight and I do not wish to deceive or be deceived.

COCHISE

October 27

Experience may be our best teacher. But it is faulty reasoning to invite certain experiences just so we can learn. This is no different from intentionally doing something wrong to see if we can be forgiven. No one should take such gambles. If we have already survived some of our gambles, then we have reason enough to quit. We get by with few things that will not have later effect. Overall, what we put into life is what we get out. If we put in wrong, we get wrong. Believing we are invincible is great if we are on the right track. Gambling is not the right track. Gambling is foolishness, and our being so sure of what we can do is dangerous in the light of all we have to watch out for in these times. Think about it.

I wish to send a little message to my people. Tell them that I am dead.

SATANK

October 28

Who doesn't long for a dear and trusted friend? There is one. It is our own inner-person that cares enough never to betray us. It is that untainted spirit within us that waits for us to recognize it, to love it. It is the real of us—our perfect pattern. It has never been too fat or too thin, never smoked too much, never overindulged in anything that would hurt us. It renews and revitalizes our entire being for it has the power to bring healing to every memory—to give us a whole new purpose. Until we tap this inward friend, we are only operating on partial power. It is the Life of Life, our saving grace and our reason for living.

Men must be born and reborn to belong.
STANDING BEAR

October 29

When we are forced to think for ourselves it is a good thing. As much as we want to depend on someone else, we are our own responsibility and we need to know how to handle it. Having someone to rely on is comforting, but it can become a reason not to think and weigh and learn. Sharing responsibility makes good friendships. But too much reliance on other people makes us vulnerable. The Cherokee needs his tribe, loves the closeness, but he must learn the things that make him able to *a li s ga s to di*, depend on himself. We need to be able to think something through–to know our strong points and how to eliminate the weak. This makes life living, rather than coping.

If the gentlemen of Virginia shall send us a dozen of their sons, we will take great care of their education . . . and make men of them

CANASSATEGO

October 30

Echoes are reflected sounds that can so easily fool us. We are confident about where the sound originates, when in reality, it comes from the opposite direction. An echo is a sound that carries across vast spaces and bounces against a far place, only to return and return again. And so it is with gossip. The sound always returns to where it originated–sometimes more than once. This is the price paid for the use of all the space, the idleness, the emptiness, and the lack of anything exciting in the life of the gossip. The worst part, idle chatter echoing back never tells that the tale carrier had nothing to personally judge by–only that it is ridiculous that the lives of others must supply the excitement.

I will make him my friend, but I will not bend my back to his burden.

MANY HORSES

October 31

October's days are splendid with their cool breezes and pockets of warm air that touch the face as though an oven door opened briefly. The cardinal flashes through the woods and the blue jay chortles and rasps with indignant jabs at the fox-squirrel. Somewhere hidden from sight, a downy woodpecker knocks like a persistent caller. What seems relaxed and at ease, is really a time of activity–getting everything ready for the onset of winter–and loving the energy it gives. We are a little like the prairie aster that blooms until it frosts, not slacking off because of what it knows is coming. It blooms profusely until the last minute– and this is the way we work.

Our country was given us by the Great Spirit, who gave it to us to hunt upon, to make our cornfields upon, to live upon, to make our beds upon when we die. And He would never forgive us should we now bargain it away.

METEA

NOVEMBER

Nu Da 'Na 'Egwa
Big Trading Month

*I am—the Cherokee are—your friends
and friends of your people, but we do
not wish to be brought into the feuds
between yourselves and your Northern
Brethren. Our wish is for peace. Peace
at home and peace among you.*

CHIEF JOHN ROSS TO ARKANSAS, 1861

November 1

Have we gotten so shallow that we don't see the importance of the earth beneath our feet? Along with air, light and water, it sustains our lives. Far too many think that grassroots is a political word. Many Cherokees still believe the herbs and roots they take from the earth make the best food and the most effective medicine. They have more faith in what they plant and harvest than they do in the fake chicken soup that seasons so many foods in recent times. But there are even more benefits that come from the earth (if there is a patch left that has not had chemicals on it). Nervous anxiety totally disappears where people can put their hands in the soil, touch it with their feet, and lie on it. Its trees carry off toxins, its roots, flowers, and even weeds have a purpose. But we are the keepers. How are we doing?

Every part of this soil is sacred . . every hillside, every valley, every plain and grove. . . responds lovingly to (our) footsteps . . .

SEATTLE

341

November 2

A long this time in autumn, we could have a few days of Indian summer. It is a tranquil time of warm sunlight with a bit of haze and soft breezes from the south. This is a token of childhood when bunches of sweet onions were hung on the garden fence to dry and pumpkins and squashes were in colorful piles. We would love this time to last longer—even anticipate that it will. But it is not likely that anything stands still at this time of year. It is too serene, too satisfying not to pass quickly. Maybe it teaches us the give and take of daily life—whether it is the weather or learning to be flexible where people are concerned. There are the pleasant days that we enjoy so much—and then there are those stormy days where we have to hunker down and ride it out.

A furious tempest continually sweeps the crown of the mountain . . . the adventurer . . . even if he escapes . . . (may be) whirled through the air by its fearful blast.
SLUSKIN

November 3

The fields that now lay cool with dew were baking in the sun only weeks ago. Change comes swiftly and what seemed forever suddenly ceases. The trees have changed from green to all shades of *ga ga ge*, red, and soon they will take on brown and russet. Even the birds that stay over winter have changed their songs, so that it takes experience to identify them. Hawks whistle ominously and owls hoot when clouds hide the sun. Nature is slowly settling down for a rest. Only man tries to keep up a relentless pace. So much that was hidden can now be seen. The view has widened with every fallen leaf. Little treasures, a burr acorn, an owl feather, a pretty rock, are more easily found on the path. It is autumn and life has already begun to renew itself for another time, another season.

I love the land on which I was born, the trees which cover it, and the grass growing on it. It feeds us well.

COMO

November 4

Individuality colors life. Our moods have color, our clothing, our skin-tones, our ideas. We were not created to be all alike, but we were created to be ourselves—to fill a place that no other person could fill. The earth would be a dull place if every hill and tree and valley were in a line and nothing could ever be different. If everything had one drab color or was totally flat, we would follow suit and be just as dull. No rule exists that we have to be like everyone else. We don't have to follow trends and do unwise things because someone else is doing them. Our lives are separate entities—apart from the crowd. It is our *a du da lv di,* our personal responsibility to keep self-respect, without question.

God Almighty has made us all.
RED CLOUD

November 5

If we ignore the beautiful and look on down the road for some future time of happiness, chances are it won't be any different. Perfect times are brief intervals between the ordinary. They create an illusion that life should be lived on some mountain top ecstasy. But we are not made to be out of this world. Our minds and bodies couldn't take it. To the Cherokee, an afternoon of fishing on a quiet, smooth running stream is a mountaintop experience. It is all to do with what we feel a need for—what means satisfaction and feeling well. The high and the low are connected. Most of the time we live in between—but that middle ground can be as rewarding as the highest plane.

The trees, the animals, are all where He has stopped, and the Indian thinks of these places and sends his prayers there to reach the place where God has stopped and win help and a blessing.
OLD DAKOTA WISEMAN

November 6

Physical strength does not comfort an aching heart any more than a sharp mind eases an aching body. But spirit has it over the other two, because it brings comfort, ease and uplifts. And we need it all. We are almost certain to have more interest in one part of us—mind, body and spirit. But if we spend all our time developing that one part to the exclusion of the others, we are going to wind up short of balance. To be really fit is to be able to depend on ourselves for anything humanly possible. We are multi-faceted and when we *i da tli ni gv si,* do our best and call on the Great Spirit, we have it all covered, and we have perfect guidance as well.

We have listened to all you have to say, and we desire you to listen when any Indian speaks. . .

PEOPEO MOXMOX

November 7

Natural doubts will come to our minds. They are familiar and will slip in on the coattails of an everyday thing. And then, they begin to nag. We can't afford to dally with doubt. Doubt can nag until it wears us down to a nub. At first, it just suggests lightly that something could be wrong—then, what if it is? And eventually, it surely must be because we feel it so in our spirits. Little seeds of *u tla si dv*, doubt, are like little grains of yeast that go into bread dough. As soon as they warm up, they begin to expand the loaf until the pan can no longer be seen. It is all so subtle.

Long Hair (Custer) came . . . they said we massacred him . . . Our first impulse was to escape . . . but we were so hemmed in we had to fight.
CRAZY HORSE

November 8

Looking back can create guilt where none should ever exist. No doubt, everyone has things they wish they had not done—but in most cases, we did what we could at the moment. Chances are that if we are spending time in regret, we are not giving ourselves to what we are supposed to be doing at the present time. It would be a shame to waste any more time on what we couldn't do in the past—and probably couldn't today. We all have something in common. The present time. From here on, we can look forward. We can still do something about our lives and stop trying to hold back, or *a da yo s da ne di,* hinder the good work we can do right now.

There cannot be two occupations in the same place. The first excludes all others.

SHOOTING STAR

November 9

I t is amazing how nice people are when we get to know them. Someone who seemed to be the most unlikeable turns out to be the very one we enjoy the most. Taking time to know others doesn't always seem important. But wonderful friends and excellent opportunities for happiness pass us by when we do not consider them important enough to know. The Cherokee people have a tendency toward *u de ho sa ti,* which means they are inclined to be shy or bashful about pushing forward. Just a little effort in reaching out to draw someone to us can be one of our most rewarding experiences. Friendship is a two-way avenue and we each have a responsibility to go part way.

This gives us great joy, for we now consider that we stand upright before you and can speak what we think.

SA-GO-YE-WAT-HA

November 10

Autumn nights, especially those of the full moon, are as breathtaking as any sunlit morning. Not even noonday brightness can compare to this peace and solitude. At moonrise, there is a velvet hour of quiet when only the largest stars are visible. The bare limbs of the great *tsu s ga* (oak) etches shadows on the ground, a lacy pattern of leafless beauty with clearly defined lines. The dark cannot hide the graceful beauty of the night, the deep, silent slumber that commands everything on the move to do it quietly. It is rest to the spirit to be a part of the quiet world, which is a joy forever.

My heart is filled with joy when I see you here, as the brooks fill with water when the snow melts in spring . . .

PARRA-WA-SAMEN

November 11

As children we scurried along some hidden path like rabbits, and thrilled to special hideaways that we were sure no one else knew about. Something in us never really grows up. We still cherish a moment of solitude away from the beaten path, *ga nv nv i*. The feeling may come in a crowd where everyone is a stranger who expects nothing of us. It may come as we walk in the woods where nature's wildlife becomes very still or totally ignores us. Or it may be behind closed doors where noise is shut out and peace reigns. Wherever or whatever we require to make us feel the comfort of solitude, it is first begun in the heart with a feeling of contentment. It is a willingness and the capacity to enjoy a secret place—like the rabbit runs of childhood.

I was warmed by the sun, rocked by the winds, and sheltered by the trees as other Indian babes.

GERONIMO

November 12

Intelligence, *go hu s di-ge sv,* is not always on the side of the dominant, nor weakness on the side of those who are dominated. Circumstances have often dictated where a person is in life—and will continue to control us until we perceive the lay of the land and change it. Some have thought we put ourselves into certain positions to be forced into learning lessons we may not have learned in an ordinary way. But we are becoming more and more aware that these things are planted in our minds to make us more manageable. What do we need to know that cannot be taught outwardly? Who is the teacher? We must be wise not to fall into the negative flow that can be poetically worded to entice us into sinister plots. It is not ours to dominate or be dominated. Ours is to love others—but we cannot do it until we have learned to love ourselves.

To clothe a man falsely is only to distress his spirit . . .
STANDING BEAR

November 13

We cannot let fear of making mistakes keep us from finding out what we can do. Only those who do nothing can avoid making a mistake—and even then, idleness is a mistake. The first step is hardest. But with every effort, the potential increases and confidence gathers. When we waver, it is natural instinct questioning if we are on safe ground—and whether we should go on. It is at our point of greatest questioning that we should gather our faith and force and move into new higher levels of self-confidence. Nothing can stop us when we know we have what it takes. Our reward is not just winning alone but the new reservoir of strength and spirit that is our resolve to do better and better.

In your actions and in your conversation do no idle thing. Speak not idle talk neither gossip. . . and do not give way to evil behavior.

FIVE NATIONS

November 14

A view of the hills lying shoulder deep in a thick blanket of fog has widened, and the barelimbed beauty of November woods is revealed. November changes the land drastically. The carpet of colorful leaves no longer rustle underfoot. The cardinals and titmice are here, but their songs are reserved for spring. Owls call early in the dark woods, and coyotes yip and wail their evening songs along the blue-crested hills. A walk in the woods is peaceful and solitary. Water harps play beneath the ice in a shallow stream. A doe's indignant snort warns that some unknown intruder is disturbing her feeding time. It is strange how common it is—common and old, but so rare and so new.

The many moons and sunny days we have lived here will long be remembered by us.
KEOKUK

November 15

Those who claim to know tell us we have to hear and say something as much as twenty-five times before it sinks into our hearts and becomes a permanent memory. But don't we know that once is enough for some things? We recall certain incidents in vivid detail—not always to our good. Why is it important to be able to recall? Some things should be clear to us, because we are ruled by what we have in our subconscious minds and hearts. And we have a lightning-fast talent for mentally scanning our memories for grudges and all things associated. Pleasantries are second-best for instant recall. It reminds us of Emerson's comment that when civilized man built his coach, he lost the use of his feet. When we store more grudges than happy memories, we lose the use of our right to be joyful.

Once I was young, my sons, and thought as you do now . . .

WASHAKIE

November 16

A midnight sky in November is a sight to behold. Nothing compares to the clarity of the limitless night sky aglitter with so many stars as to appear more like a gossamer scarf thrown across forever. We take so much for granted. The common beauty of everyday life, the sweet sleep, *ga lv di,* and quiet breathing the night offers. It seems that whatever knocks loudest gets our attention, and all that delights and comforts us slips by without our seeing it. Now, while the night sky is so spectacular, it is a gift of the season to look up and know that we are spirit-freed and unlimited. Not even the immense universe and the glittering stars created for us can compare to the stars in our hearts and what has been prepared for us.

My heart is glad and I shall hide nothing from you.
SANTANA

November 17

We tied a rock to my dresstail when I was one and a half. I cried, and my mother scolded her little brother. I could not bear to have him scolded, I loved him so. I backed up to him to have the rock tied on again. This was an uncle whose language was so colorful it was not acceptable in more genteel circles. But no man has commanded the respect and love of every person the way he did. He was an unmerciful tease, a friend in need, a giver of unappreciated nicknames, and he stood a head and shoulders above men of intellect. When he left us, hardened oilfield workers and little grandmothers cried unashamedly. He was *udu ju*, uncle, to many nieces and nephews and worlds of friends. To me he was a devoted, loving and precious friend. Can I ever measure up to such standards?

Little mountain is now dead. He did all he could to make peace.

SANTANA

November 18

The first touches of frigid air have cleared the sky and brought a stillness to the land. Long ribbons of southbound geese break into several gaggles, their cries carrying over the valley. The sound alerts us to stop and look with wonder at the changing season. Blue haze hangs in the cleft of a distant hill. On sunlit days it changes to rose then beige and near white. Sunsets are vivid and alive, streaking the sky with deep reds like hot embers that fall to the horizon and glow like the hearth in evening. But a cool moon rises over the eastern hills with all the power in serenity and peace that the sun has in riotous color. Just at that breathless moment between day and night, a quail calls. It is the simple closing of another day, a time to settle in and enjoy the peace of home.

Tell them how we loved all that was beautiful.
AMERICAN INDIAN

November 19

Our grandmothers told us that pretty is as pretty does. We may not have understood all they meant, but neither did we forget. Their words came back to remind us every time we erred. At one time, pretty meant clothes, how we did our hair, and how we handled our social graces. As time went along, we came to know it also meant how we carry ourselves, how we behaved in bad times as well as good. But then, maturity gave us another view that spoke of dignity, flexibility, a sense of self-respect and self-restraint. Pretty means honor and principle. It means caring about others and respecting them even when we do not agree. High values and reverence have made people more handsome, prettier, and under pressure, they are worth their salt!

I have promised the friendship of my tribe. . . I respect that promise. I cannot lie. . .
    WILD HORSE

November 20

Peace of mind is a jewel looked for in the worst of times and in the best of times. It is the feeling we get when we turn from a busy highway to a secluded spot along a country lane. Peace is suppertime when the sunset gilds every window and a quiet contentment makes man and nature akin. It is a warm bath, a soft pillow, a shaft of sunlight that touches the spirit. All these things make a difference, the kind words, the gentleness, the sleepy midnight song of a whippoorwill. But most of all, it is hearing something we believe when it is hard to believe in anything. It is knowing that things can work out, peace does come and life is worth living. There *is to hi ae se s di:* There is peace on earth.

The ear of the great Master of Life, which is still open to my cry, will be penetrated with the invocation of blessing. . .

SHAWUSKUKHKUNG

Thanksgiving time means the first hard freeze, the first spitting ice to rattle the dry autumn leaves. Early morning frost crystallizes grasses into rods of light. The last bit of bright color is gone from the woods, and the last walk has been taken without gloves and a scarf. But it also means family, *si da ne lv hi*, to the Cherokee. Tradition holds true in keeping a common thread with other times and other persons. We remember them with love and appreciation. We cook the same food, continue the same good-natured bantering and chaos with children underfoot. With the flow of activity, some moments can be stressful— but then, someone recalls earlier times. The young ones say what it meant to them. Suddenly, tradition takes a tighter hold—and no one minds.

So it is with Wakan Tanka. We believe that he is everywhere, yet, he is to us the spirit of our friends, whose voices we cannot hear.

CHASED-BY-BEARS

November 22

We fight feverishly for equality and freedom to do something that in the long run serves little purpose. In other times, we bargain with everything precious without the slightest knowledge about what it is costing. We feel like birds in a cage with only inches of space to fly. It is exciting to look out at the wild birds on wing and think how much we would love to spread our wings. And yet, a bird on the wing has no protection, no loving care, no regular feeding. And then we stand on the edge and look in a window and wish someone cared for us. If only there were someone like that for us to lean on. We are out in the cold—but free. The very things that pin our wings also help us to grow, *a dv hi,* and with wisdom we learn how to fly, *ga no hi li.*

Do you think I am a child seduced by trinkets?
    CRAZY BEAR

November 23

Busy hands can rest a turbulent mind. Work eases tension and sweeps confusion and regret out of mind. A lighter heart eases stress and lets good humor heal the spirit. Learn to change channels. The mind can *ayiha*, pick up on the world's invisible broadcasts to upset the more serene spirit. Awareness is the best defense. As soon as something tries to come in to cause trouble, it should be rejected. Be cautious in feeding the mind. Thought is sensitive to trouble, opening like the petals of a flower to receive, without regard to what it is. Be the head and not the tail. The head leads; the tail follows. The head thinks and knows happiness. The tail only follows.

All the headmen and braves are happy.
    SANTANA 1857

November 24

S ince *Di Ka No He SGi-Di Go We Li SGi* is a Cherokee, it is a curious thing why she was chosen to wear a Pilgrim costume in the school Thanksgiving play. Someone thought a little white apron and a prim little hat was proper for this dark-skinned child. But who has not stepped out of character at some point. Is it not true that unknowing people cast us in roles we couldn't fit in a million years. And as strange as it seems, they may never learn how wrong they were. At a time of counting blessings, we can say it does not matter what costume someone tries to fit us with. If we know who we are and the Great Spirit knows our voices, who can separate us from our real identity? Only we can—but we won't.

Never has the earth been so lovely nor the sun so bright, as today. . .

NIKINAPI

364

November 25

Our friendship has been strong through many seasons, but this time brings you to mind so vividly. Why must we rely on such changes to remind us that we are friends, not acquaintances. All is important—the way we laughed together, the times we comforted each other, the tears we shared and the deep understanding. This time, like no other, enhances those things that make us akin. It surely must be the hope, the vibrant life of power unused—the power of love to transcend time and space and lost connections. It is the same power, the Great Spirit, that is all good, all peace, all ours by divine right. It is a precious partnership between friends.

These beads are a road between us. Take hold at one end, I will at the other, and hold fast.
    COMO 1793

November 26

Sisters are such special people. They can outthink, outdo and love us better than anyone in the world. They stand with us in difficult times, rejoice with us in the good times, and talk to us with loving words to lift us up. The Cherokee calls these special people their *a na da lv*—beloved sisters. Sisters never complain when we get lost in time and space—never forget to welcome us home. Sisters don't have to be blood kin—for what does that matter when the relationship is stronger than ancestry. Love transcends so many dry places and makes us family by choice. What could be better than to be a beloved sister?

I consider them as my own. Their wishes are our wishes, and what we get I hope they will get.
RUNNING ANTELOPE

November 27

Since our early years, we have learned that age is a state of mind—and that sometimes we are several ages all at one time. The number of years we have lived means nothing. Some never achieve poise and wisdom. Some seem to be born with it. No one cares how old we are if we are projecting something worthwhile that defies age. When we are comfortable with ourselves it reflects agelessness that only grows better with the years. Age, the Cherokee believes, includes the many stages of life to measure wisdom. If our minds are kept flexible, our bodies will be lithe and easy—and if our thoughts are rigid, our bodies will reflect it. We either grow and mature beautifully or we lose our flavor—like rare spices left in the wind.

These people who want to go there will get old pretty soon.

TOOKLANNI

November 28

Time and again, we have seen help come from the most unlikely places. But our minds are set on certain things, certain ways that something can be done. Healing must come from a pill or a shot, love must come whether or not we are lovable, joy must come from something that happens—not from within us. We refuse the best help because we do not see it in a familiar light. If it is not the right color, the right shape, the right sound—can it be ours? Can it possibly help? It is possible to relearn the natural ways of doing things when we open our eyes and our hearts to the inner-knowing, the wisdom and peace of the Great Spirit. There is more to living than our eyes can see, more than our minds can perceive—but it is right here now, waiting to make the difference.

There are the springs of the Great Spirit. . . To bathe in them gives new life; to drink them cures every bodily ill.

ARAPAHO INDIAN GUIDE

November 29

Some of us build bridges and go in search of rivers to fit them. Those who stew and fret about every little thing are building bridges. How many bridges do we build that we never have to cross? How often do we refuse to see the bright side because we don't want to give up our view of what could happen? How many expect to feel depressed and lonely and done-in? It may seem at times that we are frozen in space and nothing can change, nothing can go right—but that is only an opinion supported by negative ideas that have already attracted the wrong experiences. Build a new bridge—back over the troubled water, and cross it confidently. Don't run back and forth, but tear it down and refuse to build any others.

His brave warriors will be with us, a bristling wall of strength.

Seattle

November 30

Stand still. No matter how hard it is, stand still and let what has already been started work itself out. Don't talk, don't touch what has been set in motion. To press and push and double check the works when it is all normal and moving can be damaging. *Ga to gv*, stand still and keep a single eye. If the principle is sound, it will do a good work. When we believe in what we are doing and we have done it to the best of our ability, then it is time to keep our hands off and spend time blessing. Reach past the present moment to a new vision. See the end result. See it completed successfully. Never mind the in-between—only say it is working well.

They speak of the mysteries of the light of day by which the earth and all living things that dwell thereon are influenced.

PLAYFUL CALF

DECEMBER

U Ski'Ya
Snow Month

Given the proper incentive, no mountain, it seems, is too high to climb, no current too swift to swim, if one is a Cherokee.

GRACE STEELE WOODWARD

December 1

Early mornings have supernatural qualities, unreal, yet more real than most things we put stock in. So many beauties, so many things that happen within our sight are overlooked and unappreciated. They pass without notice and will continue for the sake of the land—whether they are seen or ignored. Nature thrives in place where people give up. It has defied verdicts placed on its very existence—and still creates breathtaking views. We have the same abilities if we can keep out the greed and grime that pecks at our minds. The fact that we are *u ne na i*, wealthy, escapes us when we litter the grass ablaze with dew gems and scatter debris in every sparkling stream.

The Kiowa braves have grown up from childhood, obtaining their medicine from the earth.

SATANA

December 2

The law of the echo is at work in our lives. It is the law of give and take, what we put out we get back. It is not limited to material things but to every facet of our lives. What we say, how we treat others, how we stretch the truth, and how we set out to hurt someone's character, these things and more have everything to do with our well being. But they are too often thought unimportant, judged to be *u lv da le s gi*, which in Cherokee means the absurd or foolish, but the *Tsalagi* lives by the law of the echo. He knows it is not foolish. We cannot be too careful about what we send out. Can we be as careful of our words, our actions, as we are about polluting the atmosphere with carbon dioxide? The result is the same—it just comes in different packages.

You will. . .use all means to persuade any tribe to come in for the purpose of making peace, and when you get them together kill all the grown Indians and take the children. . . sell them as slaves to defray the cost . . . .
CONFEDERATE GOVERNOR JOHN R. BAYLOR 1862

December 3

In our estimation, most other people are happy, some supremely happy. But are we thinking this because we are making comparisons? Are we asking how someone else can be so secure, so at ease, when we happen to know their unforgivable acts in the past. Envy and resentment of other people are weapons against us. They keep our eyes focused outside ourselves where nothing is ever quite the way it looks. We have no idea of what is going on in other lives, what their thoughts are and what they have resolved. There's great contentment in minding our own business. We can correct what needs correction, make amends if we need to—but let the questioning go. We cannot know how good or how bankrupt another life is—but we can know what controls our own.

Do right always. It will give you satisfaction in life.
WOVOKA 1889

December 4

The land is quiet and serene along a country road in this season. Natural sounds, the crow, the rapping of the red-headed woodpecker, and the ring of an axe in the woods, carry easily over cold airwaves. Like voices with no accent, no soft edges, all are heard clearly at a distance. Even now, the land is colorful. Tufted grass, nature's rose-colored silk, dances in the breeze. Evergreens break the tans and grays at the pond's edge and dot the shadows along the timberline. The flowers may be gone but Indian mullein carpets the ground in secluded areas. Winter has a delightful beauty, red sunrises, magnificent sunsets and layers of blue, deep blue, and purple along the horizon. Quail, like school children in single file, cross the meadows to feed. Peace sounds no alarms, and all is well.

When winter comes on, you can take shelter in the woody bottoms . . . find meat for yourselves and cottonwood bark for your horses . . . it is the right place.

ARAPOOISH

December 5

Our hands tell who we are. They are believed to be perfect subjects of the mind. As physical labor shows in the callouses on our palms, so does gentleness or greediness or strength. Nothing else expresses human behavior in so many ways. With our hands, *tsu no ye ni,* we work, play, love, threaten, show joy or grief. Sensitive symbols of faith and friendship, our hands draw to us everything and everyone we love. Marvelously made and directed by the mind's eye, the mind's ear, and the heart's desire, our hands continually express our lives. An abusive hand is from an abusive mind. But the gentle touch does exist—even for those who have yet to experience it. What words cannot say, the hands can express with all tenderness and love.

Now we shake hands and make peace . . .
SPOTTED TAIL

December 6

The instant that something offends us, we are off the track. Resentment surges through us and nothing is going to please us. We learned how to walk and talk and rely on people—and to mistrust them as well. We have learned how to think, how to rate people and systems—and how to berate them. We form opinions, set up values, decide how far we will go and how little it takes to reach a goal. And somewhere along the way we find that others have done the same things and will not respect our opinions. We are offended—*e s ga-nu li s da ne lv gi*. Taking offense creates a weak link. All our gifts, talents and skills must be united so that we are centered and poised in our own consciousness. When we take offense, we are not shut away from living, but our mouths, our eyes, our thoughts are aware of the weak link.

It has come to me through the bushes that you are not yet all united; take time and become united. . . .
    BIG BEAR

December 7

The easiest thing in the world is to look at someone and say what we would have done in their place. Yet none of us knows what we would really do until we are in their place going through the same things. We are meek in our thinking, but prepared to do battle if we need to—or so we say. How inane to talk a good fight and not even be able to stand up for what we believe. How reckless to think we know what we would do. Self-sufficiency is a mark to our good— but has it ever been challenged? This is the reason we need the compassion and support of other people— we can hold each other steady in times of stress and trouble. Together we build courage and pass it around to anyone who needs it—and still have plenty to spare.

Our knifes were ready, and the heart of Black Hawk swelled high in the bosom . . .
    BLACK HAWK

December 8

Humility is what we think other people should have. But from the instant we think this, we need it even more. Humility is knowing we are nobody when it looks like we are somebody. It is believing we are somebody when it feels like we are nobody. Humility is being sufficient, but lacking pride in sufficiency. It is knowing grace—and knowing we did nothing to earn it. Humility is being modest, but not resigned. It is in the deepest sense—kindness. It is being plain folks that love and care about everyone around them—never taking into consideration whether anyone loves and cares about them. It is *yv wi-a ne hv*, humanity, in its absolute best clothes.

That is the way with us Indians, goods and earth are not equal. Goods are for using on the earth.

YELLOW SERPENT

December 9

Take away the plastic, the film, the artificial and give a small boy a stick to dig in the dirt, to whack the water at the pond's edge—and you have given him happiness. Show him deer tracks and the handprints of a raccoon, and you give him curiosity. Boost him up to the lowest limb of a tree and he can take the next one with vision. Show a small boy something other than cartoons, sing him songs that are not commercials, teach him gentleness with small animals and other children, and you have given him a life laced with love and kindness. The best part of sharing an hour with an exhuberant little boy is that he gives back so much, shining eyes, imagination, questions without end, and laughter at nothing and everything. It is an hour well spent and will be remembered. Hopefully, in later years, he will recall that it was spent with Grandma.

It does not require many words to speak the truth.
CHIEF JOSEPH

381

December 10

While it pays to be cautious, very often our skepticism is surpassed only by our ignorance. When we can't believe in anything that doesn't figure in dollars and cents and other tangible benefits, then life is all on the surface. More of life is invisible than visible. We draw on the invisible the way we draw on a bank account, seeing nothing of the workings but getting results. We believe our money is in the bank, not expecting it to be where we can see it. When we need it, we call for it. The Cherokee believes the Great Spirit has a great many other things, health, peace and happiness to name a few, in the bank for us. It is our part to keep what we have balanced, to add to the strength of it with faith, and to be grateful for it. But until we call for it, using the right name, it remains where it is.

Indians . . . know better how to live. . . . Nobody can be in good health if he does not have all the time fresh air, sunshine and good water.

CHIEF FLYING HAWK

December 11

Why are we willing to settle for less than what we can have? Why do we consent to live on the fringes of other people's lives, standing on the outside looking in with longing eyes? We are not meant to be fringe people, starving when there is a feast prepared for us and waiting. It is like owning a mansion and living in a closet, catching the crumbs when we should be sitting at the table. A few moments spent on the edge of life is sometimes thought to be worth the hollow times. But we are more apt to be lonely, *u hi so di,* the Cherokee calls it, peering inside than having an expanded view of the whole outside. There is more pain in imagining what other people are doing than in looking at our own potential and going toward it. Fringe people have tremendous capacities for living— and with a little evaluation and change they can use them all.

There was a time when I had a choice.
RED EAGLE

December 12

We are different—you and I. We have differences in background, education—creeds perhaps. But more basic than that, the shape of a hand or an eye, the working of the mind. Knowing how we differ, why do we question the variances of opinion, attitude, faiths and how we look at life in general. What could be more tiring than seeing ourselves in whatever direction we turned? If we had nothing to challenge our views, would we ever think more deeply, rise higher? It is not our differences that make the difficulty in the world but our prejudices against difference. Yet none of us controlled his or her beginning. It is ignorance that makes us rebel against other races, other creeds. And ignorance is trouble itself.

The Great Spirit made the white man and the Indian. He did not make them alike.

DAYKAURAY 1829

December 13

Protection is not a weapon or a locked door—or even a ferocious appearance. Protection is from the inner person. It gives an invisible sign that this person is not vulnerable but a presence that defies *sedani*, or evil. Security is not easy to define. It is not foolhardy and it is not overbearing. But it does have a calm poise that even animals respect and bad people avoid. It is a strength that anyone in his right mind will not put to a test. These are days that speak of caution. Take nothing for granted and wear the protective armor of faith and firm decision. Agitators are as cowardly as they are smart enough to know that you do not prey upon someone who understands the situation and is ready.

I do not want war, but want to make friends.
SANTANA

December 14

We cannot see everything from beginning to end. Life is too large to see that far. Sometimes it seems we have to give more than we receive. We sometimes have to reach beyond what we really want to do, or take part of someone else's load rather than see them break down. Sometimes we forgive more than we are forgiven, and work harder to believe in the goodness of the Great Spirit. We may lose sight of God, but God never loses sight of us. And then there is a burst of sunlight, a new day when we know that giving more is blessed. The scales balance out and we see that we cannot get less than we give when the gift is our best. It is impossible. We cannot love more than we are loved.

If I have these and kept back the best no one would believe I was in earnest. I must give something that I really value to show that my whole being goes with the lesser gifts; therefore I promise to give my body.
MATO-KUWAPI

December 15

The secrets of Christmastime give ordinary work special meaning. The sights and sounds of the season mean getting ready—preparing for the celebration. We hear woodcutters busy with their saws, yelling back and forth, and the thumping of firewood as it is thrown into the truckbed. A thin spiral of smoke rises above the treetops as brush is cut away and burned. Fallen leaves tumble into the blaze as though some great hand swept them all in one direction. Christmas has always taken some of its delight from the woods. Burr acorns and puff balls and clusters of red berries festoon the wiry vines on the rough trunk of the hackberry. Breath hangs in a misty vapor and a cardinal flashes red through a light misting of snow. A joy to be, a joy to see.

We acknowledge first the goodness of Wakan Tanka . . . we are sure his spirit lives . . .
    CHASED-BY-BEARS

December 16

Someone said humorously that there is one thing money cannot buy, and that is poverty. But it can. It doesn't take money to be the richest person in town. Anyone that has survived an ordeal, where to merely exist is important, knows what it is to be rich. It is life seen through the heart—and for them poverty doesn't exist. Prosperity includes many things. Simply being well in body, mind and spirit tops the list. But seeing the change of seasons, touching the faces of those we love, breathing fresh air, or breathing freely, is wealth unlimited. The Cherokee expression of wealth is *nu we hna v i,* but personally, it is the right to be free, the right to pray, the right to one's own decisions. And that should enrich all of us.

In the last place . . . we are bound . . . to watch for each other's preservation.

CANASSATEGO 1742

December 17

One of our basic needs is to be accepted. We fear rejection and somehow get the idea that we are worth only what someone else says we are worth. We can't allow their experiences to put limits on who we are. Looking for approval is a vicious circle. An outsider can be suspect—simply because he is an outsider. And every person has to realize that self-respect and self-acceptance precede what others may think. Confidence is knowing who we are, heart, mind, and spirit, and never allowing that confidence to cause us to put someone aside because he lacks standing. The Cherokee believes we should not *a da de hu to di*—insult the Great Spirit by criticizing one of His creation.

Many times we have been laughed at for our native way of dressing, but could anything we ever wore compare to the utter foolishness of the steel-ribbed corset?

STANDING BEAR

December 18

Initiative is the will to win. It is the decision to begin right where we are, the self-starting push that gets us over the hump in the road. It is the smile and the quick step that gets us past what seems wrong. It is the ability to see a rainbow when others are crying over the rain. Initiative is a new surge of bravery that makes us stand up straight and use our heads and hearts and not fall into envy and fear. It is a new burst of strength that understands what it takes to get going. And the best part of self-motivation is to follow up the will with good work, with more faith and more courage—that this time, this time, we are going to strike gold! This time is a new time, a new heart, a new person that will not wilt in the face of opposition.

The Great Spirit puts a shadow in your heart when you destroy. . . .

JOE FRIDAY

December 19

Sadness clings like dust particles, and makes us think there is no other way to feel than sad. But what makes us sad? Is there something tangible that we can deal with? Or is it just everything—and yet, nothing in particular? At times, there is a sorrowing of the soul, the deep-seated knowledge that all is not well, and things are getting worse. No one respects anyone else and when will it cease? How can we be happy when there is so much wrong around us? This is our chance to be a seed of happiness, a spark of hope, a star that someone can look to and follow out of a dark place. If we fall into a trap that we are supposed to be sad—then, we are no different from the unknowing ones. Sadness is a symptom that is contagious—but so is faith and cheerfulness.

I am heard now by all Indians, and they are pleased, and have said to me, Brother Teedyuscung, you are promoting what is good. . .

TEEDYUSCUNG

December 20

Some things deserve to be remembered—others to be forgotten. Many of us fail to think and speak positively because our memories are too good. We need both—remembering and forgetting—to keep us balanced. Remember some of what was wrong so as not to repeat it—and forget some of what was right so not to park by it. Every day is a matter of picking up and putting down, catching hold of what we want and letting go what we do not need. When we are happy, there is nothing worse than recalling vividly the miserable times. And when we are miserable, we know that we can remember being happy, then we have the capacity to be happy again. Remember with understanding—and sometimes remember to forget.

When the sun goes down, he opens his heart to God, and earlier than the sun appears on the hills, he gives thanks for his protection during the night.

CORNPLANT 1791

December 21

The sense of touch is the most improperly used of all our senses. There is nothing more dear than the touch of someone we know we can rely on or with whom we feel secure. And there is nothing less appealing than the heavy hand that can't get near without pressing or insisting on contact. Many times, such persistence is insecurity and the need to be noticed—sometimes it is ignorant boldness. The less tender concern a person has in his nature, the more he requires of others. All of us need to be touched, to be treated with kindness—but everyone has not developed a caring touch. If it is not good, it is known instantly and alienates. If it is a thoughtful and warm touch of kinship, it is soothing, the way love touches.

The Great Spirit is looking at me and will hear me.
CHIEF JOSEPH

December 22

There is something about a Christmas sky when the night is clear and still, and the stars are bright enough to light the way without the help of the moon. The countryside lies quietly under such a sky, peaceful and serene, with only the softest hoot of a distant owl. Even the cattle move slowly in the herd or stand quietly around a stack of hay. Nature can soothe the land and give us peace if we can let it be—if we can tune in to the silence and feel the tranquillity that smothers the rush of too much activity. Christmas was a gift to us. When we hear the chimes play music out across the rooftops, it is balm to the soul. And then we know what it means, that it includes us in the new birth.

Indians love their friends and kindred, and treat them with kindness.

CORNPLANTER

December 23

This is the time to talk kindly to ourselves. When time and tinsel begin to depress, some time alone is not a bad thing. And there's nothing wrong with being alone. Who is better company than we are? Who is more important to our well-being? Never say it is not worth the trouble to celebrate alone. When we are good friends with ourselves, we are good for others. This is the time to wrap two gifts. Put time and thought into the selection and into the paper and ribbon. Then give one of them to someone who most likely will not have a gift—and save the other to open later. The Cherokees are a close-knit tribe, but every person knows it is important to enjoy a time of perfect solitude and celebration. We need to know that when we all come together we will have something to offer—ourselves.

I must give something that I really value— therefore I promise to give (myself) my body.

Chased-By-Bears

395

December 24

All that has been a part of the important past is a part of this more important present. We are bits and pieces of who we were yesterday and all the many yesterdays—and we are stronger persons with new eyes and new hearts. This is the day for which all preparations have been made. It dawned like any other day—but it came bearing gifts. This is the turning point, the place where we begin to see over the hill and around the bend. A new path comes into view and there is no longer a need to look over the shoulder. What might have been cannot govern or grieve us. Better, happier and more joy-filled times are, the Cherokee says, *e gi ni yo ha*: they are looking for us. And they have found us.

The reason Wakan Tanka does not make two birds. . . or two human beings exactly alike is because each is placed here. . . to be an independent individual to rely on himself.

OKUTE

December 25

E ach of us have known kindred souls. They are those special persons who understand exactly how we feel and what we think and need. They seldom talk about it. Such relationships have no need for discussion. Their quiet companionship is balm to the spirit and enough without words. Wherever we are, we meet these special people who have known loneliness and have heard the empty echoes but have not let them spoil anything. They are what the Cherokee calls, *a ga-li s gv ti tia.* They are on the sunny side. Now they mark the way for us, telling us that life is good and we are going to do well—and what we really need to hear, we are not alone. Then, we can reach back and take someone else's hand to lead them across the lonely places.

The monitor within my breast has taught me the will of the Great Spirit . . .
    SENACHWINE

December 26

There is always a way. Solutions will not come when we are hanging onto the problem for dear life. When we back away and get a better perspective, the chances are good for more than one solution—we can choose. We are known for insisting on the wrong answer—believing the way we see it is the only way. But if something knocks our hand loose from its clinched position, ideas can flow out like water from a hose. When we cease to heave and sigh and begin to let our imagination work, it can reach into areas that our ordinary knowledge doesn't have. It should be an act of anticipation—a great expectation that the Great Spirit is putting the answer where we can find it this very moment.

You sent for us; we came . . .
      TALL BULL

December 27

Who is to say what is holy? The *Tsalagi* (Cherokee), believes that whatever the Great Spirit made is holy. A mountain, a tree, the whispering stream is holy. So much has been lost in the translation that we are inclined to pick apart what another thinks is holy and good. Our limitless connection to all that is holy can give us a great comprehension of peace and health and all that is needed. If we follow the much-trodden path, believing that to be holy we must be poverty-stricken, downcast, and victims of an angry God, we are fooled. The idea that we can earn our way overburdens us. When we put it all down and turn toward the Light, sweet grace is poured upon us.

The Great Spirit bade him (Pontiac) to be seated: I am the Maker of heaven and earth, the trees, lakes, rivers, and all things else. I am the Maker of mankind; and because I love you, you must do my will.

December 28

This is America—a place where people can agree to disagree and not lose their standing. An American often represents the pooling of different cultures into one unique individual—many times with one blood running more strongly. Each adds character and strength to a nation of people. We are great for calling each other names. The Indian has been called drunken, lazy, and easy to dupe. Before the Europeans came, he knew nothing about liquor, he lived well, ate the healthiest foods, and wore luxurious furs all winter. He often went south in cold weather, and summered in the mountains. He loved his people, his land, his God, his peace. He is the sovereign native-American Indian.

In all your official acts, self-interest shall be cast aside. You shall look and listen to the welfare of the whole people and have always in view, not only the present but the coming generations—the unborn of the future Nation.

DEKAWIDAH 1720

December 29

Country sounds abound on a cold winter evening. A cow bawls, dogs bark, voices carry across the frozen land. Evening brings the comforting thought of home. Wood for the fire, soup for supper, a cat stretching on the window sill and waiting to be fed. And winter sunsets are the essence of all that is beautiful. The last few minutes before the sun goes down, it fires the horizon with live embers, hazes the hills with blue, and then turns deep purple, red, and gold—gilding the treetops and reflecting in window panes. If there are a few gray hours in winter, far more are filled with thoughts of home, sharing, and time to enjoy it.

I beseech you . . . by everything you hold sacred and dear. . . arise to the dignity and grandeur of your honored position as the father of your gallant little band, shake off the fetters of the Bad Spirit. . .

KEOKUK 1832

December 30

There are times when we forget the road we have been over together, how difficult it was, and how good. Undoubted loyalty has thrived between us. We know we can depend on understanding and kindness, but most of all forgiveness. We have laid aside anything we did not understand until it came clear, yet we have not excluded others or forgotten their importance. The Great Holy Spirit wrote it in our contract to take special care, to load every rift in life with good thinking, good acting, and good words. From the beginning, we have planted good seeds. Now is the time to share the harvest. We will walk on paths of peace and broadcast to others that it is well with us.

It is my duty as your chief to be your father while in the paths of peace, and your leader and champion while on the war path.

KEOKUK 1832

December 31

The woods have been a place of enchantment, a world of lacy patterns and mysterious stillness. The snow- and ice-covered limbs of huge oaks form intricate patterns against the sky, and ribboned lace, white on white, lies across the frozen pond like tiered ruffling. It is the only time of year when the white bark of the stark cottonwood blends with the landscape, and the bright red cardinal becomes a striking contrast. Nature's patterns are etched in ice and in us. There are places within us that are as soft as silk, *si li gi,* and as polished as silver, *adelv-negv.* We have designs in our souls, varied in color, solitary, enlivened with warmth and love—and beauty we often view as illusionary. But sometimes it is the illusion that is most real.

You promised us that the weather would be clear and that your children should have so much silver that when they looked at each other they would look as bright as the rising sun.

OTTOWAN CHIEF

Notes on the Native American motifs in *A Cherokee Feast of Days*:

halftitle page and page 205, July: rayed concentric semicircles from pre-Columbian Mississippian culture (Proto-Caddoan), ca. 1200-1350, excavated at the Craig Mound, Spiro, Oklahoma.

page 9, January: prehistoric Hopi pottery design, polychrome, ca. 1375-1625, from northeastern Arizona. Recorded by Jesse Walter Fewkes in 1895.

page 43, February: a Kwakiutl killer whale design, ca.1900, from an ancient seafaring culture of British Columbia.

page 73, March: pottery motif, ca. 1890-1910, from the polychrome painted and polished ceramic tradition of San Ildefonso Pueblo, New Mexico.

page 107, April: Zia polychrome pottery design of a doe with encircling floral motifs, ca. 1880-1890, Zia Pueblo, New Mexico.

page 139, May: Prehistoric Mississippian Issaquena stone disk with entwined snake motif, ca. 1200-1350, redrawn from the 1926 archaeological record of Calvin Brown, Moundville Site, Alabama.

page 173, June: prehistoric Hopi pottery design, polychrome, ca. 1375-1625, from northeastern Arizona. Recorded by Jesse Walter Fewkes in 1895.

page 239, August: pre-Columbian Moundville stone disk redrawn from record of Clarence B. Moore, 1905.

page 273, September: Southern Plains Cheyenne ledger drawing, ca. 1878-1880.

page 305, October: Chemehuevi (Arizona-California) basket design, ca. 1900.

page 339, November: Zia polychrome pottery design, ca. 1880-1890, Zia Pueblo, New Mexico.

page 371, December: motif from prehistoric Mississippian Indian culture, ca. 1200-1350.

Assistance in locating and identifying Native American motifs courtesy of Dr. Edwin L. Wade.

Index by Topic

Index by Source